THE
ENTREPRENEUR
WITHIN

THE ENTREPRENEUR WITHIN

How to FORGE innovation-led growth
by embracing the inner entrepreneur

MARK ROBERTS

UNICORN

CONTENTS

FOREWORD

DAVE FOREMAN

MANAGING PARTNER,
PRAETURA VENTURES

AS A VC, WE SPEND OUR DAYS searching for the best ideas. Ideas that make our lives easier, faster, greener, cheaper or better in some way. In a world where the rate of change is ever increasing, our ability to form and execute new ideas is the only true source of competitive advantage.

And many start-ups threaten established businesses because companies lose their ability to innovate as they grow. Simultaneously, start-ups often fail because they cannot scale. The venture ecosystem exists because of our collective failure to 'think' en masse.

Recent history is filled with incumbents suffering from stagnant thought. Mocked in business headlines, their collapses are often viewed as gross oversight. The industry shames those unable to see threats to their hard-earned monopolies. Yet these issues repeat time and time again; because being innovative is hard.

Through decades of finding and backing exceptional founders and helping them build great businesses, Praetura has learnt that a team's ability to continuously innovate through problems will ultimately decide whether they survive or thrive. Whilst this may seem obvious, an innovation-led approach requires discipline and must be prioritised. Few leaders can truly maintain this over time. For every new hire, you must work even harder to give them room to innovate. To kickstart UK productivity and create more globally consequential companies, we must improve our ability to create, package and ship new ideas at scale.

Leaders have long searched for structures that maximise productivity, often with limited success. Research shows autonomy, mastery, and purpose drive motivation. We have found that if an organisation truly embraces an innovation-led approach, another unexpected benefit surfaces. By raising the bar and challenging staff to innovate, their sense of autonomy and purpose drastically increases. It's no secret that our lives are improved when we can make our own decisions. This approach becomes effective when channelling this energy towards a common goal and equipping teams to excel. Both small improvements and big leaps can benefit your team. As an existing or emerging leader, your job is to live it and help your team translate this formula into their day-to-day.

As for innovation strategies, look for inspiration wherever you can find it. Great ideas are often other people's concepts applied to new fields. Evolution not revolution has led to some of the most important companies shaping our lives today. This is what has driven the thinking behind *The Entrepreneur Within*.

Mark's perspective is rare and recent. A man who scaled a business in a tough sector from a fairytale 'two mates in a garage' story to $200m in revenues. Having achieved a celebrated exit, his capability led him to achieve even greater scale through his role as an 'intrapreneur' at his acquirer AB InBev. Few have been able to earn their stripes in both little and large organisations. For this reason, Praetura trust him with our most precious asset – our portfolio founders. As an active mentor, he helps some of the best and brightest minds in the north of England try to make their mark on the world.

Focus. Originality. Results. Growth. Ecosystem.

These are the distilled elements that have led to Mark's consistent successes. Harbouring a natural tension whilst creating a process to follow, we will also be looking to apply his tools in our businesses.

Many overcomplicate the world of venture. As one of the fastest-growing venture businesses in the UK, we know the formula is simple. We look for great ideas, great people and great execution, but we pursue this honestly and relentlessly. We believe Mark's methods will help us continue to create firsts for our industry and 'do the impossible' where others cannot.

We hope you enjoy the book as much as we did.

Dave Foreman

INTRODUCTION

*'Our greatest glory is not
in never falling, but in rising
every time we fall.'*
CONFUCIUS

A TRUE STORY

The words from the board were very encouraging.
It was a green light. We had the ambition. We were ready to
challenge the market, to shake things up. We knew that by
serving the customers better, the whole business could grow.
We had to find a better way, and we had tremendous ideas
of where to start.

I joined the bank full of optimism. After all, I was
appointed as the head of innovation for a major division.
It was my job to be optimistic and creative. We had an
exciting innovation pipeline, and we ran headfirst into it.

Two years later, the same problems remained;
I admitted defeat and reluctantly moved to a more
traditional marketing role. Looking behind me, the projects
we developed gradually died. The early promises – full of
hope and encouragement – ultimately seemed disconnected
from reality. The whole team had done everything possible
to inspire innovation from within the bank, but we were
stifled at every stage. We were constrained by budget
challenges, by committee timelines, and by specialist teams
incentivised to point out every reason why a new approach
could not work. Red tape bound us down. Our job was to
run, like entrepreneurs, headlong into solving the problem,
but instead, we were running through committees of treacle
(to coin a collective noun).

I've led innovation portfolios in multinational companies, been a scale-up entrepreneur, worked as an intrapreneur within a global corporation, and as a venture capital investor. In every venture, I began to see the same underlying problems.

As an entrepreneur, I relished the freedom that small business brings, but I also experienced the challenges of having few resources as well as the growing pains of scaling fast. And then, in a large corporation, I was again reminded of my time at the bank, attempting to slash my way, Indiana Jones-style, through the jungle of constraints, my hat left on the other side of the door.

I began to realise that there are common threads that impede innovation within organisations of all sizes. I shared my thoughts with dozens of business leaders, all corroborating my experiences. You, as our innovator-in-chief, our entrepreneur within a business, will no doubt have shared similar pain.

This book is the culmination of decades of experience innovating inside and outside established businesses. It's the culmination of dozens of interviews with business leaders who have made things happen at companies including Nike, Sony, AB InBev, Apple and many more. You'll hear from many of them in this book. I've studied where innovation has worked and, perhaps more importantly, where it hasn't.

I started collating these ideas and experiences alongside interviews, research and thoughts, and the result is this book, *The Entrepreneur Within*. FORGE®, the methodology that this book outlines, has become my playbook for innovation. I hope it will guide you through the challenges of innovating within an organisation, understanding where to focus, how to scale up, and explain how to keep an entrepreneurial mindset alive within any organisation, no matter how much jungle undergrowth or how many swishing poison-tipped arrows there are around you.

IS THIS BOOK FOR YOU?

Do you recognise any of these pain points?

FOCUS

» We can't articulate a coherent strategy for growth or differentiation.

» We're too reactive to market pressures and competition,
  not creating our own path.

» We're falling in love with the solution, not the problem.

» Our new initiatives don't fit in with our mission.

ORIGINALITY

» We struggle to have genuinely creative thoughts.

» The ideas we do have don't cut through.

» We have too many naysayers who block progress.

» We don't seem to prioritise the most promising ideas.

RESULTS

» We're scared of failure.

» We don't test things quickly enough, or don't know
  when things are good enough

» Decisions are taken without the right data.

» We're not quick enough to back projects that show traction.

GROWTH

» We struggle to get new initiatives beyond a certain size.

» Our decision making is starting to slow down.

» Some of the team are becoming disenfranchised.

» We can no longer see the forest for the trees.

ECOSYSTEM

» We're too internally focused.

» We don't have access to the very best talent.

» We're on the back foot with the latest market developments.

» We take on all the innovation risk ourselves.

If you recognise any of these challenges, the FORGE playbook can offer a new perspective on how to move forwards and unlock growth.

Innovation is critical for business growth, and, ultimately, success. You innovate or die. But how do you foster a mindset of innovation within an organisation that might have lost it? Is the current approach not working? FORGE will also diagnose the reasons why. I'll show you how to overcome the hurdles and create an environment where entrepreneurs within a large business or organisation can be empowered.

SO WHY LISTEN TO ME?

I've always worked in innovation, from my first job out of university to, well, right now. Innovation is at the heart of everything I do, pretty much every day of my working life. I've read everything I can find on the subject and put the theories to the test in large corporations and high-growth start-ups. I advise companies and organisations across the world on innovation, how to foster it and, crucially, how to maintain it. I've worked in innovation roles my entire career, in organisations of all sizes. I'm an industry advisor at the University of Oxford; I've chaired regional economic development panels, advised governments and embarked on trade missions, all with innovation at the core. I've been an entrepreneur, building my own business and selling it to a multinational. I've also worked within corporations leading disruptive technologies and ventures, for example, at Procter & Gamble, Lloyds Banking Group, AB InBev and Leeds City Region Local Enterprise Partnership. I'm now an angel investor, operational partner of a venture capital company, non-executive director and, yes, let's say it, author. My career, crucially for this book, has straddled the entrepreneurial start-up, as well as working for a large corporation.

And that juxtaposition is the essence of FORGE. It is about fostering and maintaining an entrepreneurial mindset while navigating the restrictions of a large organisation. You have the big business resources (yay!), but also the big business red tape and complexity (boo).

I've first-hand experience of the very common challenges that innovators within a large organisation face. It can seem to intrapreneurs and innovators that they are seemingly stifled and stymied at every stage, regardless of the board's understanding that innovation is required. I also saw how a lack of innovation gradually leads to a decline in the business. If a company of any size is not innovating quickly enough, you can guarantee the competition is.

As an entrepreneur, I co-founded Beer Hawk with a good friend. It was an e-commerce business that grew out of a shed and two laptops into a company with more than £90 million in revenue and a 200-strong team in less than a decade. Along the way, we sold our business to AB InBev and eventually helped integrate it into the mothership.

An innovation paradox became clear. New ventures within large organisations are increasingly constrained by processes and long-standing culture, red tape and stakeholder management. Large companies tend to be conservative, motivated by short-term profits. When an innovative business grows, it becomes more efficient, but this limits innovation. This is not the right environment for a venture requiring a start-up mindset.

On the other hand, a venture that needs to scale must implement the rigour and efficiency of large-scale business to be sustainable, all the time maintaining an innovation stream to ensure it stays ahead of the competition. These are traditionally opposed. Entrepreneurs are brilliant at innovation but often need help to scale; corporations scale effectively but struggle to innovate. It's why so many start-ups fail and why so many innovations in organisations fail to gain traction.

Overcoming this paradox is what the FORGE methodology addresses. I call it 'becoming ambidextrous'. It's about mastering the skills of both innovation and efficiency.

HOW TO USE THIS BOOK

This book is split into two parts: firstly, Growing Pains, and then FORGE, my methodology for innovation success. The first part of this book offers the context for innovation. It analyses why innovation can be such a challenge, and why it is critical for a business to survive. It addresses why it matters to be innovative, why business ventures become less innovative over time and why large organisations usually kill innovation or suffocate the creative process. I talk about the challenges you, as the innovator-in-chief, face. I discuss why companies become like this.

In the second part, I explain how we rise to these challenges and turn them to our advantage to ensure innovation is present at every stage. And, ultimately, how to create a sustainable, scaling business with longevity, an environment where people are happy to work, and that does good for the world.

FORGE has five chapters: Focus, Originality, Results, Growth and Ecosystem. It is the order by which innovations should be developed. I say 'should' because we know that's not always the case. Chances are you'll be at a different stage of the venture, or different stages with different innovations. While I'd suggest reading the book in order, you can absolutely dip into the chapter that addresses your needs most clearly. However, I do suggest you read Ecosystem soon, it is an essential element of all the other stages.

Throughout, you'll see a series of Tales, Traps and Tips. These are interviews with some of the world's most interesting innovators. In these pages, they offer inspirational stories, as well as hard-earned advice, the successes they had, and failures you can avoid.

I've also included some well-known examples of business success and failure from some of the world's biggest companies. Full transparency: I wasn't there for those decisions, I have no idea exactly what was going on in the head of Steve Jobs, for example, but these cases do illustrate a point, a principle, and that is very worthwhile.

Most of all, *The Entrepreneur Within* is designed as a playbook to be well-thumbed, to have scribbled notes in the margin, and to sit open at your desk, ready to guide you towards the next step.

This book offers decades of learning from more than a dozen people – innovators who have made mistakes and discovered patterns of success. It can act as a shortcut to becoming The Entrepreneur Within.

THE TRUE REASON FOR THIS BOOK

I'm passionate about innovation. I love the buzz of being part of new ventures, I love hearing how they succeed. When businesses grow, when they scale efficiently, it improves the lives of people, it improves the economy, it benefits everyone. But here's the real crux: innovations can change the world. I believe that if we solve the problems of innovation, we can solve at least some of the problems of the world. That's why I wrote this book.

Mark Roberts, 2025
Harrogate, Yorkshire

PART 1

GROWING
PAINS

STAYING AN ARTIST

'Every child is an artist;
the problem is staying an
artist when you grow up.'
PABLO PICASSO

LIKE A PIECE OF ART, all business ventures begin with a blank sheet of paper. There are no rules; there are no processes. It's creator mode. This is the time to embrace the problem and find the solution. It's a thrilling moment. You are drawing your future.

Give a child paper and pencils, and they embark on a similar creative journey, unencumbered by the 'expected way of doing things'. They interpret what is going on in their free minds. It's quick, often scruffy; it's colourful; it's energetic; it's creativity at its purest. What is in the child's mind is what appears on the paper before them. They're not adhering to the rule of thirds; they're not thinking about contrast or perspective, about light direction or colour palettes. They're simply creating.

Now ask an adult to draw the same thing – say a house – and if they're as artistically talented as I am, making a terrible attempt at the brief. If I were drawing in front of a peer, I'd be a bit embarrassed. I'd ask myself questions about style, form, colour and size. I doubt it will be free-flowing. I'll have a handful of half-remembered 'rules' and a lifetime of societal norms; I'd have a tang of fear of failure and abundant self-criticism. I'd also, no doubt, have a deadline looming and a phone buzzing. This will not be my most creative moment.

The business venture, the new product or service, the thing that will make your customer very happy, begins with that blank piece of paper. A start-up is like a child, unburdened by rules and corporate regulations and free from financial obligation. There is little need to please stakeholders, procurement departments or the legal team. There is complete flexibility. And then there's speed, plenty of speed.

That said, there is often no money in the bank, no customers, no established routes to market, and even if there were, there would be no products to sell. Oh, there is no IT support either.

A large corporation is a grown-up, acting, hopefully, in a very grown-up way. Risk is mitigated, finance is in order, processes are in place, and regulations are strictly adhered to. But as Picasso so succinctly said: 'The problem is staying an artist when you grow up'. If he were writing a business book (and thank goodness that was never on his agenda), he'd have written, 'The problem is staying an entrepreneur when you grow up'.

It's easy to fantasise about early-stage businesses. It's the ultimate freedom. But ask any entrepreneur who's moved from a piece of paper to a company, and while there are rose-tinted reflections, the reality is that it is hard.

From the moment a new company is born, and the trading name is chosen, the business is constantly in flux. No organisation is ever static, but early-stage ventures take this to the extreme. Many companies never make it out of what I call the 'Ignition' phase, but those that do can experience a blaze of growth which can be one of the most rewarding, if terrifying, periods in the typical business life cycle. This is especially true once you move from a one- or two-person company to employing staff. And once you are growing, it's time to start innovating again, and quickly. For those ventures that can reach a substantial turnover, there is too frequently a tendency for leaders to pat themselves on the back, sit back, and wonder why the company is stagnating. They get stuck, really stuck. And it's actually at this phase where many businesses fall, whether a start-up with twenty people or a product team within a huge organisation. Ask someone who is trying to innovate within a large organisation, launch a new product, lead an innovation team, or just see how to make things better, and you'll get a similar response. Innovating is hard; when that's in a grown-up company, it can be harder still. That's why I wrote this book.

This book provides a methodology for creating the ideal conditions that will help innovation take hold, whether you're employee number 2 or 902. We will look at techniques to instil the founder's mindset required to innovate, highlight the traps businesses fall into when trying to innovate, and showcase the success stories to inspire your business venture. We'll hear the pitfalls to avoid and secrets to follow to maintain innovation at every level from those who have been through it, and my own experiences.

Innovation is inspired by a great number of reasons, but the environment needs to exist to encourage it.

THOSE AWKWARD TEENAGE YEARS

This first section is called 'Growing Pains', and with reason: the transition from start-up to successful enterprise is seldom smooth. All founders hope their 'baby' will grow into a flourishing adult: successful, wiser and wealthier. Sure, there'll be the terrible twos, the stroppy toddlers, the belligerent eleven-year-old and the oh-so-tricky teenage years before slowly calming down, settling into a comfortable house with an armchair, disposable income and a garden to maintain.

But it's not like that. Businesses are, of course, different to people. Many of us will have missed those formative years of a company and joined directly at the point of having a little middle-aged spread and that lovely garden. And that's often the point you're asked to shake it up. To pull a product or service out of the bag, to supercharge growth. But first it's important to understand exactly what the growing pains are that companies of all sizes experience.

First, as Led Zeppelin succinctly put it, there's a communication breakdown. As companies or business units grow, communication across the board is more complex. Informal chat is less effective, and it becomes harder to distinguish the important information from the noise.

Along with increasing size comes a loss of agility. Decision-making often slows down, the organisation becomes less responsive. The need for an approval process, or at least 'alignment', is necessary. An added complication is the fear of losing what the company enjoyed in the first place. That's the fear of losing the agility, speed and the culture. A start-up environment is thrilling, quick and relatively flat in its structure. As the company grows into adulthood, the founding team loses influence as new hires are rapidly onboarded. This often puts a strain on those there from the beginning.

One of the growing pains we see is operational inefficiency. Roles become ambiguous as new team members overlap responsibilities. The initial 'all together' ethos without clear, formal job descriptions means there can be a lack of clarity. And what works for a small team might not scale effectively.

I'll go into more reasons why businesses develop like this as they grow; it's one of the key challenges you will face. It's about understanding how it needs to grow efficiently, and – if my editor would let me put this in big bold caps, I would – continues to keep that entrepreneurial mindset alive. This is the challenge this book addresses. Show me a company that hasn't experienced it.

THE CREATOR MODE SWITCH

So, how do we keep this entrepreneurial mindset alive and thriving within an established organisation? You see, with the very best of intentions, people like to optimise things. To tinker. As businesses grow, there is a requirement to improve processes and make the entire system more efficient. It's necessary but problematic.

Every stage of the business life cycle presents benefits but also poses challenges, often significant ones towards the latter stages. The problems experienced during rapid growth are very different from those associated with stagnation. The business must adapt at every stage to survive. It's also about how a business adapts to shifts in trends, economic turbulence, as well as major upheaval.

Decision-making processes, communication and governance systems evolve as the organisation grows. A successful corporate organisation has typically mastered these. In the first part of this book, we'll discuss how and why these changes happen. Still, it's worth pointing out now that as a company moves through these stages, the environment for early-stage innovation usually becomes increasingly desolate. It's critically important to look for ways to balance existing revenue streams with developing new ones to achieve sustainable profitability.

Constant change, without direction, can mean that an organisation can spend a lot of money and considerable effort without generating meaningful progress. Growth is critical. Businesses, to survive, need to be able to drive efficiency *and* innovate. They need to become ambidextrous. This book is about finding ways to be efficient *and* innovative.

EMBRACING THE BUSINESS LIFE CYCLE

ALL BUSINESSES GO THROUGH a very similar life cycle.[1] It's been written about at length. The key challenge is how a business can spark new growth when experiencing decline. Understanding this life cycle is integral to maintaining growth and building a sustainable business. The diagram I've built for this S-curve shows when innovation needs to happen for the business to break away from the potential decline; it's called jumping the curve. Spoiler alert: you need to be innovating early, not towards the end when the decline looks ominous.

This book isn't concerned with the first two phases of this S-curve. That is your start-up business and there are plenty of books about that. Instead, it's about how we can ignite new growth in an established business.

A word of warning: revenue as an indicator lags far behind action. Innovation efforts need to start sooner, much sooner, than most businesses realise.

Most successful business ventures will typically pass through five distinct phases:

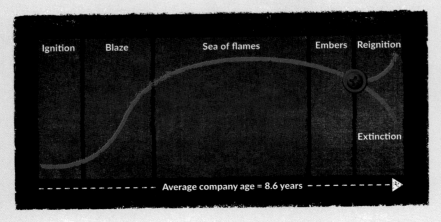

1. IGNITION

The exciting, but somewhat terrifying bit, is the start-up phase. The emphasis is on developing the value proposition and validating the concept – are people buying it? We then need to progress by testing the riskiest assumptions and finding market traction. And while this is called ignition, it's also the time many new ventures fail to find the spark in the first place or are snuffed out before too much money has been spent.

2. BLAZE

Product-market fit. If you've hit the Blaze phase, it's usually a sign that you're on the way to achieving the fabled 'product-market fit'. Life looks pretty good. You've survived start-up. Widgets are flying out of the warehouse, sign-ups are exceeding expectations. It's likely the internal processes haven't quite caught up with the pace of demand, so things might feel quite chaotic. Of course, the other scenario at this stage is for the new venture not to survive, becoming another innovation failure statistic. Let's call that the blaze of glory!

3. COMBUSTION

The growth phase or, ideally, the sustained growth phase. The break-even point came and went without as much as a bottle of sparkling English, and it's starting to generate positive cash flow. Sales, while maybe no longer being the talk of the town, continue to increase with the ebb and flow of the market tide. However, at risk of sounding like a horoscope, there are likely to be some darker clouds forming. Maybe there are new competitors, demands for new capital investment, and pressures on gross profit margins. This is the time to prioritise making the next big innovation.

4. EMBERS

You've now been around for a while. People know the brand, but new sales are more challenging to achieve, profit margins continue to thin, and the pressure on cash flow is real. The length of this decline phase can vary considerably, but unless reinvention is achieved now, an eventual market exit is inevitable. Urgent attention is now needed to extend the business life cycle. You definitely better be innovating.

5. REIGNITION OR EXTINCTION

Uh-oh. We're in decline or, euphemistically, transition. In this stage of the business life cycle, sales, profitability and cash flow often decline in unison. The only way here is down. Or up. Choose reignition. Reignition requires innovation. And quickly. It's already usually too late. Your current offering is no longer fit for market. Innovate or die.

THE INNOVATION
PARADOX

HOW GROWTH STIFLES CREATIVITY

'You can't allow tradition to get in the way of innovation. There's a need to respect the past, but it's a mistake to revere your past.'

BOB IGER, CEO OF THE WALT DISNEY COMPANY

THAT WORD 'INNOVATION'

Innovation. Yes, 'innovation'. That word. The one that gets batted around in meetings, in articles, in your brain as you're about to fall asleep. Are we innovative enough? Was our latest product innovative? Is our marketing innovative? What on earth does 'innovation' actually mean anyway?

Thousands of definitions have been offered up. For those interested in a spot of etymology, the word's origins lay in the mid-sixteenth century and emerged from the Latin *innovat* meaning 'renewed, altered' and from the verb *innovare*: *in* ('into') and *novare* ('make new', from *novus* 'new'). But it wasn't until the 1950s that the word took off in popular diction.

The word innovation has increased by a factor of nine over the last seventy years, according to Google. Incidentally, at the same time, the word 'invention' has dramatically declined since the end of the Industrial Revolution. There are subtle differences. Invention, perhaps obviously, is defined as the action of inventing something, typically a process or device. Its Latin roots are closer to 'discover' or 'finding out' than 'renewing'.

Personally, I prefer the original 'discovery' concept. That's because I think of innovation as forging previously unseen connections. That's 'forging previously unseen connections'. I'm repeating it because it's important. I do, however, offer two caveats. First, we're talking about innovation within a business here, so there needs to be a commercial benefit. Secondly, while this definition could cover all new process improvements and marketing tweaks, we're intentionally focusing on more transformational innovation for this book. Specifically, new ventures that are a significant step away from the core business (see the Innovation frontiers section which follows). This is not to say that the FORGE Methodology in Part Two of this book is not helpful for all innovation projects, but that some elements will deliver more significant benefits to projects with more radical intent.

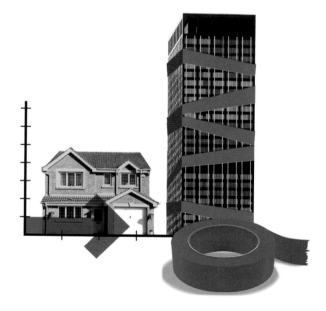

INNOVATION FRONTIERS

'INNOVATION FRONTIERS' SOUNDS LIKE a fancy term for striding out into the Wild West firing off ideas into the wilderness, but really, it's about how different the innovation is to the core business.

As you can see from the diagram, I find it very helpful to separate *where* to play from *how* to win.[2] As you can see, the level of risk increases the further away from the core business that you go.

WHERE TO PLAY
New products
New markets & existing products
Existing markets

TRANSFORMATIONAL
ADJACENT
CORE

Existing markets
New markets & existing products
New products

HOW TO WIN

CORE: OPTIMISING THE EXISTING OFFERING

Innovating at the core delivers incremental improvements for existing customers or improvements to the company's existing offerings. The goal in optimising the core is to innovate and expand core offerings, to be able to gain efficiencies by either improving performance or reducing costs. It's extending the business life cycle. It can, and should, be part of everyone's job, regardless of their function.

ADJACENT: EXPANDING INTO NEW AREAS

This expansion could involve finding new customers in adjacent markets or developing new use cases by adding new products or services to existing propositions. The aim is to leverage existing capabilities while exploring new opportunities that are still close to the current business.

TRANSFORMATIONAL: DEVELOPING BREAKTHROUGHS

This type of innovation aims to develop new breakthroughs and invent new propositions for markets that might not exist yet. The objective is often to create significant shifts in the industry landscape, and it involves much more radical change. And risk. But there is much more potential for reward.

This book is concerned with those innovations beyond the core. So how do you know where to play? And how are we going to win? Thinking about frontiers in this way poses five important questions for a new venture:

» How far away are we from our core competencies?
» How close are we to our existing audience?
» Can we apply similar solutions that we have used in the past to solve our problems?
» How much investment will be required?
» How confidential should this proposal be? Will there be a significant first-mover advantage?

These questions are all explored further in Part Two.

THE IMPORTANCE OF INNOVATION-LED GROWTH

IN THIS EVER-CHANGING, ever-expanding world, innovation has become more than a nice to have; it is essential. Full stop. It is critical to business growth. It's the Holy Grail – the actual one, not in a Monty Python way. Everyone knows that, right? Right? How many business leaders do you know who have called for less innovation? According to McKinsey, 84 per cent of CEOs believe innovation is critical to business growth.[3] And let's also be clear: getting good at innovation has benefits beyond growth and beyond profit.

INNOVATION DRIVES GROWTH AND BUSINESS PERFORMANCE

Growth makes everything easier. It helps if you're trying to raise investment, recruit and retain talent, or have momentum in the sales pipeline. A growing business often attracts additional cash contributions, offering reinvestment opportunities alongside healthy profits. There's a warm glow of positivity about the business's future.

However, over time, most products and businesses experience a natural gravity impacting top-line revenue. Without action, revenues will typically shrink.

So, let's look at what happens when a business isn't growing. If the top-line revenue graph looks slow, stagnant or curving downwards, the rational response is to optimise profit first. How do we do this? Typically, we would start interrogating every expenditure item on the P&L and consider options for boosting margins. Enterprises embarking on such 'efficiency measures', including overhead reductions, can significantly improve the bottom line.

There are plenty of examples of companies following this path to profit optimisation with great success. In fact, this can lead to core innovation as new approaches to increasing efficiency are explored. It can be especially true for businesses that have reached peak demand or experienced supply constraints. Now, the game becomes optimising value from stable revenues.

However, the most visible impact of the strategy of profit optimisation is on people, the company's culture, heart and other vital organs. If a business is seeking to optimise profit, it's all too frequently at the expense of people. The headcount is chopped. It's often the first thing a new CEO considers when coming to reverse the decline in the company. But that can, figuratively, feel like heads are rolling out the door, still blinking. It can be catastrophic for the people who are made redundant and very unnerving for those remaining. The good people in the business will spend much more time on LinkedIn, hastily clicking different tabs when anyone walks by. I could point to dozens of examples here. In 2023, Twitter (X) underwent a massive cull and started haemorrhaging its greatest minds. Turn on the news, and job losses are a constant thread, whether it's a high-street retailer, car manufacturer or steel works.

Innovation can change all of this. Innovation unlocks new revenue streams, it attracts new audiences, it adds value (and profits) to existing customers, it increases brand value, it opens up new networks, it hones the business structure, it changes the mindset of employees, it improves products, it solves problems for customers, for businesses, for the world.

It makes growth sustainable. Businesses must innovate, reinvent and renew. Shoots of new projects should constantly rise around the core business. We never know what is coming, and we need to be prepared. Growth is the only way to arm ourselves against uncertainty.

INNOVATION BUILDS THE MUSCLE
TO THRIVE IN UNCERTAINTY

One million users. In the tech world, that's one of the most tracked metrics. In 1999, Netflix launched; remember those DVDs coming through the post? It took three and a half years for one million people to wonder where they'd put that little envelope. In 2004, Facebook took nine months to reach a million. Instagram: two and a half months. One million users were agape at Chat GPT within five days. In 2023, it took two hours for one million people to sign up for Threads (we can't be sure how many went on and wondered what it was for and never used it again, but that's not the point). If you were wondering, the telephone took seventy-five years for a million people to dial Mum.

Look at another metric: the average company lifespan on the Standard & Poor's 500. When this index that tracks corporations on the New York Stock Exchange was formed in 1957, the same year that Disney's IPO took place, the average lifespan of a company was sixty-one years. Today, it's a few months under eighteen years.

These statistics run together and make an obvious point: we are living through a time of elevated uncertainty and are witnessing more rapid change than at any other time in history. Technology moves at a pace that outruns commentary, and the resulting disruption to established industries is happening quicker than ever before.

An organisation's only armour against this rapidly changing environment is the ability to innovate. It counterbalances the change, or, ideally, it is the change. However, the organisational muscle for responding quickly needs to be strengthened. It must constantly be challenged, and not just in a crisis. The business world is awash with examples of disrupters, some of whom rocked established industries: Airbnb and the hotel industry, Uber and taxis. Compare Kodak with Fujifilm. While the Eastman Kodak Company is still licking its wounds, providing 'industry-leading products and services for commercial print, packaging, publishing, manufacturing and entertainment', as well as 'retro cameras', Fujifilm (tagline: Value from Innovation), as early as the 1980s, recognised the shift to digital and diversified into healthcare and materials, as well as imaging.

It's remarkable to imagine that Lego faced bankruptcy in the early 2000s. Still, according to Brand Finance, a blend of smart offloading and innovation led to its becoming the most powerful brand in the world, above Apple and Ferrari. Crisis can be a precursor to success. In fact, half of all Fortune 500 companies were created in a crisis. This esteemed list includes UPS and General Motors (panic of 1907), Fortune magazine, United Airlines and Walt Disney (market crash of 1929), Hewlett Packard (Great Depression, 1935), FedEx, Microsoft and Costco (oil crisis in 1973, then recession from 1973 to 1975), LinkedIn (2002, post-dot-com bubble) and Airbnb (2008).

And it's not just small, nimble companies that can succeed in a crisis. If – and it's the big IF we address throughout this book – large companies with the innovation muscle will prosper. Just think about responses to the Covid-19 period. Some businesses stagnated, panicked, and relied on government handouts to survive (many failed), while others pivoted and thrived. According to global management consultancy McKinsey & Company, organisations that maintained their innovation focus through the 2009 financial crisis outperformed the market average by more than 30 per cent and saw accelerated growth over the next three to five years.

We will have a successful company if we build the ability to change, flourish without certainty, and be prepared when disruption comes. As Alan Kay – chief scientist at Atari and formerly a member of famed research organisation Xerox PARC – frequently said: 'The best way to predict the future is to invent it.'

INNOVATION HELPS ADVANCE OUR MISSION AND DO SOCIETAL GOOD

There are huge problems to solve in the world. Just turn on the news. Some are old problems still searching for a solution, and some problems are waiting in the wings. Some new issues are even created by a new innovation launching, which in turn sets off a requirement for further innovation. This is not a bad thing. It becomes a unique 'innovation stack', which is very difficult for competitors to copy and benefits the consumer. When this stack is closely aligned with the company's mission, it can also benefit society. Let me explain.

Jim McKelvey founded Square Payments which allowed millions of small businesses to accept credit cards for the first time. From this one problem to solve, they also had to design easy-to-use software, keep customer service costs down (by providing a fantastic service), and innovate with marketing rather than spending heavily. That one problem led to dozens of innovative ideas throughout the customer journey. McKelvey called it the 'Innovation Stack'. In his book *The Innovation Stack: Building an Unbeatable Business One Crazy Idea at a Time*, he wrote: 'The problem with solving one problem is that it usually creates a new problem that requires a new solution with its new problems. This problem-solution-problem chain continues until one of two things eventually happens: either you fail to solve a problem and die, or you succeed in solving all the problems with a collection of both interlocking and independent innovation.'

Jim McKelvey's innovation stack wouldn't have worked, however, without a clear mission. Explorers may have travelled without maps, but successful companies with a clear purpose and mission know precisely where they want to end up, even if they're unsure of the route. Importantly, they know why. This 'why' connects the growing number of purpose-led companies worldwide. Purpose, in itself, is even becoming big business. *Forbes* reported that consumers are four to six times more likely to buy, protect and champion purpose-driven companies, especially younger consumers.

One only has to look at the monumental success of Patagonia, a brand so successful that consumers wear the logo with pride because it is a brand with purpose. Lovely though the clothing looks, it's no better functioning than dozens of other outdoor brands. Instead, it is the activism and banner-waving care for the planet. It is genuine, directly making a difference, and, in terms of profit-making, it is emotive. It offers the reason to buy Patagonia above all others. Patagonia is a brand that reflects our values and is singularly clear what people stand for.

Or take Grameen Bank, self-billed as a 'Bank for the Poor'. It's a microfinance community development bank in Bangladesh where no collateral is required to get credit from the bank. It has existed since 1983 and was formed out of a community project. It's expanded rapidly and is now an inspiration to hundreds of similar projects worldwide.

Innovation can play a vital role in advancing the purpose and mission of the business. Patagonia's founder, Yvon Chouinard, undoubtedly began with an ecologically conscious ethos – he was a founding member of the 1% for the Planet organisation – but it still made new climbing apparel. Today, its activism defines the brand. It has played a massive part in its brand success while genuinely doing good.

There is also clear evidence that innovation-led growth can enormously benefit society. Growing companies, for example, can bring economic affluence to the communities where they are based. One only needs to look at the development around Bentonville, Arkansas, to see the impact of having the Home Office headquarters of Walmart located there.

Businesses do exist to make profits, but Nobel laureate William D. Nordhaus estimated that 'innovators can capture about 2.2 per cent of the total social surplus from innovation'. Turn that remarkable statistic around:

97.8 per cent of the benefits of innovation flow to society and not the business.

Let's not underestimate this. It's one of the reasons I wanted to write this book. The more companies that experience high growth through innovation make a clear and positive difference to the communities they are part of. And, of course, some of these businesses go on to solve some of the world's significant problems.

THE TIME IS NOW

THERE'S NEVER BEEN A BETTER TIME to innovate.

It's a bold statement, but I passionately believe we now have more tools available than ever to help innovation succeed. Why? Thanks to innovative technology, a product launched in Liverpool, Buenos Aires or Tel Aviv can find a global market almost overnight. Exceptional talent is a LinkedIn post away, and capital for fresh ideas is abundant. Everyone wants innovation, and the world is set up to provide it at breakneck speed.

Since the turn of the twenty-first century, you can run a successful business from a laptop in a coffee shop. There's no need to take a substantial financial risk on premises, stock or wages. Two decades earlier, the software you'd need would have required heavy investment in servers. Now, it's a monthly cost, streamed to you anywhere in the world.

When we set up Beer Hawk in 2012, we incorporated and developed an online store, secured (very) basic premises, acquired craft beers from around the world, and set up a logistics operation and payment capability, all for less than £5,000. The website was far from pretty – mainly brown – but it could handle concurrent orders, process payments and offer real-time stock control. I still had to learn how to code (bringing in a specialist freelancer for the tricky parts), and much of the design was my handiwork (eek). But it worked. And it was cheap. Well, we thought it was at the time. If we were to set up this business today, we could do it for less than £1,000. And it would be significantly better thanks to all the templates and website integrations available now for a few pounds per month.

Today, the opportunities are astonishing. Here are a few examples of what can be achieved for minimal cost and in a couple of days:

» Reach highly specific market niches in just a few clicks and for just a few dollars.
» Access the inner thoughts of leading entrepreneurs streamed to your phone.
» Find deep expertise on 99 per cent of subjects within a few minutes at minimal cost, curated for you by AI.
» Set up an online store selling multiple product categories, in multiple currencies, within days.
» Raise capital from communities of online backers and angel investors across the globe.
» Access a network of over one billion global freelancers offering over 500 specialist services.
» Automate routine tasks, from scheduling to coordinating resources, with free software.
» Produce individual products with 3D printing and other just-in-time manufacturing services.
» Discover trends from vast data sets with intuitive tools; no data expertise is required.
» Incorporate a business with a full suite of legal documents within minutes.

The best part is that many of these technologies, and many more besides (look at what Nike's Michael Steen is saying about AI), is that they all bump into one another, compounding the outcomes.

Developing a new business idea has never been quicker, easier or cheaper. And the risk of failure has plummeted to an all-time low. It's not only 'fail fast', but it's also 'fail cheaply'. Entrepreneurs no longer need to risk their houses to gather the start-up capital required to test an idea, and corporations no longer need to spend hundreds of thousands on market research.

SO, WHY THE STRUGGLE?

Remember that McKinsey study quoting the critical importance of innovation? Interestingly, the same survey found that only 6 per cent of CEOs are satisfied with their innovation performance.

There's no getting away from the facts: innovation is hard. The innovation roadside is littered with countless failures, and even accomplished innovators struggle to maintain consistent success, especially in larger organisations. Innovation remains a constant frustration for many companies.

We can throw around all manner of statistics on this, whether from new start-ups, to those on innovations within companies. And it's high. 95 per cent is at the upper rate, while other studies have it as low as 40 per cent (although not many). Most studies hover around 80 per cent and, of course, that rate differs across different industries. Importantly, definitions of 'success' also differ widely. For example, large organisations will often kill potentially successful innovations early as it doesn't meet their criteria. When I spoke to Michael Steen of Nike, he said the company had cancelled products that a hundred companies could have been founded on.

A business can fail at many things, but if they're small things and you fail quickly, it typically doesn't matter. It's more about the wasted effort and missed opportunities. The knock-on effect impacts the team and the employees, who can become increasingly disillusioned. And at its extreme, it could be an existential threat to the company. If one organisation can't innovate, you can guarantee that another can. Disruption happens, and the extinguishing begins.

So, what is the Innovation Paradox? Apart from an impressive-sounding chapter title, the paradox is simple: businesses that have experienced innovation-led growth tend to create internal systems that unintentionally stifle further innovation. By doubling down on what made them successful, a company may be threatening its very survival.

This fundamental tension in the organisation happens when creativity and control have different requirements. It pulls the organisation in opposite directions.

As I mentioned in the introduction, I've found that there are typically five categories of explanation for why things go wrong for organisations struggling with innovation. And while we don't want to strike a negative tone, it's essential to look at why organisations suck at innovation. And, if you pay real attention, you may see a rather neat set-up of the FORGE methodology!

THERE IS NO STRATEGIC INTENT FOR INNOVATION

Despite executive rhetoric, innovation is simply not a genuine priority in many companies. There may be a declaration of intent in the strategy, but it often lacks real thinking on how to achieve it. There probably is an executive who doesn't believe that innovation is essential, but I've never met one. Perhaps the organisation boasts a 'Head of Innovation', a 'Head of Transformation' or, *shudder*, a 'Head of Disruption'. More dangerous than a burning platform that demands innovation is a reasonably stable platform with a couple of small conflagrations but in a generally 'OK' state. Here, procrastination takes hold.

In *The Innovator's Dilemma*,[4] Clayton Christensen articulates the first innovation dilemma that established companies face is when a potentially disruptive technology comes along. These companies must cater to their existing customers and continue offering incremental product improvements, but, detrimentally, not make products that eat into profit margins. This approach diverts resources which could otherwise explore disruptive technologies, the ones that will ultimately keep the company ahead of the curve and ensure long-term success. What appears to be the best approach for the short-term success of the business is often not the best approach for the long term.

Companies with a clearly defined innovation strategy and those with apparent ownership of innovation at the board level will stimulate innovation and, with it, the ability to break the usual business life cycle. Companies need to focus on a particular problem and innovate around it; otherwise, they will not survive. And, yes, I said focus. That's 'Focus'. Yes, it begins with a capital 'F'. You may see where I'm going here.

THERE IS LIMITED CREATIVITY

Ideas need to come from anywhere and from anyone. Far too often, the leadership's eyes are closed; there's not the forum or the environment where daring ideas are celebrated. It is difficult for new ideas to stand out in an organisation where everyone is pressured to do the day job. Sometimes, there's just no real time to think. In the relentless pursuit of efficiency, it is challenging to carve out any organisational slack for creativity and fresh thinking; we need to be more deliberate on what not to work on. Creativity is important to shift a good idea to become a truly transformational one.

And let me repeat, the ideas can and should come from anyone. One reason creativity is rare in a company is that, institutionally, there isn't enough diversity of thought for genuinely original ideas to spark. Or it could be that those little sparks and anthropomorphic lightbulbs have nowhere to go. There's no ideas backlog to add to, leaving almost no chance for any ideas to be digested, let alone turned into an investable proposition. And once you've not been listened to a couple of times, well, why would you want to give the good ideas away? It's why good people leave to start their own business.

Even when ideas do cut through in an organisation, there is typically too much groupthink and an absence of genuine freshness for real inspiration to strike. The concept of 'corporate memory' is helpful to understand here. 'That didn't work before; why should it work now?' By their nature, existing businesses or internal business units tend to be insular, too, with external viewpoints often seen as a threat and, therefore, not added into the melting pot.

But it still shouldn't deviate from innovative concepts needing genuinely original thought to gain traction in the market. In a later chapter, I discuss creativity techniques designed to break down groupthink and instil freshness within established teams and organisations. Organisations need to build an environment to foster and celebrate creativity and originality. For the record, that last word started with an 'O'. (Duly signposted.)

IT TAKES TOO LONG FOR IDEAS TO GAIN TRACTION, OR FAIL QUICKLY

Good governance in a company is designed to promote efficiency, reduce risk, improve decision-making and encourage organisational stability. These are all important and desirable outcomes for a business, but with one massive trade-off: these processes seriously hamper the speed of decision-making and getting things done.

Nobody has ever been fired from an organisation for pointing out potential pitfalls of a new approach or suggesting that further data be sought to make an informed decision, but data (potentially too much of it) can lead to companies getting stuck. Yet these seemingly innocuous questions in a meeting can silently kill a new idea. Especially when asked by the right person. A genuinely innovative organisation must accept that failure is a natural part of the journey to success. Risks need to be taken. A different approach is required for 'new' from 'existing'.

This is not to say that validation shouldn't occur or that good governance doesn't have a hugely important role within a corporation. However, the results must be validated in the market, not in the meeting rooms of a corporate HQ. Results, as we'll see in the chapter called, yep, Results, is about rapidly testing Desirability, Viability and Feasibility.

Today, the tools to discover this are more readily available than ever, sometimes even without producing a product yet; just look at the Kickstarter and Indiegogo models.

In the FORGE methodology, results are at the heart. But it's about seeking the right data, learning from the right testing and taking the right actions based on the results.

THE INNOVATION HAS NOT BEEN DESIGNED TO SCALE (APPROPRIATELY)

A £100,000 revenue business can be meaningful for a sole entrepreneur. For a corporation already turning over eight figures, it's relatively meaningless.

Some organisations have startlingly high expectations about innovation. Is it really worth doing if it doesn't improve the annual results? For those within organisations promoting innovation investment, the lure of promising instant returns and meaningful scale is hard to resist. The reality is that most innovation takes time to scale. This doesn't mean it's not worth the investment, nor that a new launch is a 'failure'. New ventures can take more time to scale than initially thought. The person who authored the annual business plan, loaded with promises, may not be happy with the results. Nor will it help the career paths of those who led the way.

Should the core business catch a cold or require a profit contribution, the first place to look is those new ventures that haven't got going yet. It's brutal but understandable. Compare this to a start-up business, which does not have those expectations nor, frankly, an alternative. Start-ups have nothing to lose. Growth (a 'G', hello) must be accomplished, but in the right way.

NEW VENTURES STRUGGLE TO ACCESS THE RIGHT RESOURCES

Resources are more than money. They're about talent, knowledge, finance and networks. They're about having the very best people, applying specialist knowledge, being supported with growth capital and being signposted to external resources that can really make a difference.

As new ventures develop, the requirement for different resources changes constantly, and the speed of accessing these resources is directly proportional to the ability to grow. Yet it's not always apparent to those inside a venture what resources are needed, let alone what resources are readily available.

For innovators within a large corporation, it's easy to be consumed by the array of internal resources available. However, this approach can overlook vital external perspectives and market intelligence. It can miss new ideas and technologies starting to gain traction. It can overlook the knowledge and expertise that an 'outsider' could bring to bear on the challenges.

Existing companies like to boast of an 'unfair advantage' from the resources they have at their disposal in quantities start-ups could only dream of. But sometimes, having such resources at your disposal becomes a disadvantage because it can block the desire to collaborate and seek external validation with the very best minds in the industry. For this methodology, we call it the Ecosystem. It's about creating the perfect environment for innovation to spin the flywheel. It's a loose, amorphous idea, but essential for success.

THE GROWTH IMPERATIVE

Grow or die. The message is clear. We'll look at why established companies struggle to get new ideas off the ground and why the systems and processes in organisations work against early-stage innovation. We'll look at how to break out of that spiral, to fight the status quo and truly empower innovators and leaders. We are in the business of change. Businesses need to push through the growing pains. As I alluded to in the previous section, there are five distinct areas where innovations go wrong in large organisations. That is because of:

» Lack of Focus
» Lack of Originality
» Lack of Results
» Lack of Growth
» Lack of Ecosystem

In the second section of this book, you'll have the tools to help break through each of these shortfalls, no matter the size of the organisation you're operating within.

To be clear, I'm not advocating a wholesale change of business structure. Those checks and balances, as well as systems and processes, must be in place. The organisation needs to be efficient, risks must be managed, and communication must be readily facilitated. But we must also ensure that we keep the capability to break through all that, create new stuff, introduce new products, and embrace the changing world. As Erica Yong puts it, 'If you don't risk anything, you risk even more.'

In the next chapter, Becoming Ambidextrous, we investigate how businesses can keep the entrepreneurial mindset alive within any organisation.

It covers:

➡ How to foster the growth mindset.
➡ How to manage the stages of launch to scale up.
➡ Empowering the entrepreneurs within the organisation.
➡ The culture of founders within an organisation.
➡ The perfect mindset for a founder.
➡ Creating and sustaining the innovative internal culture.

BECOMING
AMBIDEXTROUS

FLEXING THOSE INNOVATION MUSCLES

*'I'd give my right arm
to become ambidextrous.'*

LAWRENCE PETER 'YOGI' BERRA,
US PROFESSIONAL BASEBALL CATCHER

STAYING IN NEVERLAND

J.M. Barrie was inspired to write *Peter Pan*, or *The Boy Who Wouldn't Grow Up*, by the children of a friend of his. The opening line of the 1911 novel is: 'All children, except one, grow up.' The children, as they start their adventure, are full of hope and excitement; this is their greatest adventure. Peter Pan, Wendy and her brothers set off together to explore Neverland. But they have to return to London. Peter Pan wants to stay in the Neverland forever, refusing to grow up. The innocence and imagination of youth conflict with the responsibility of adulthood. Peter Pan chooses not to grow up.

You're a step ahead here, no doubt. This childlike enthusiasm, yearning for adventure, and wildly creative imagination is the mildly selfish mindset of the entrepreneur and one that abounds in the heated atmosphere of a start-up. This book is not designed for start-ups, but the central tenet is how to foster that mindset in a more established business. My argument is simple to explain but fiendishly tricky to develop in real life. A business must innovate to survive, and as our innovator-in-chief, you must keep that start-up mindset alive, be more Peter Pan. The looming BUT is that you must do this within an organisation which has already grown up, become an efficient business, developed robust processes and opened communication channels to an increasing number of employees.

Peter Pan is not our model. Successful businesses have to grow up (I'm afraid), but you do need to keep that mindset. These are the growing pains, and becoming ambidextrous is my way of saying you must master both efficiency *and* effectiveness, creativity *and* control. Part Two of this book explains *how* to do that, but first, we need to know what we can extract from start-ups and bring into the world of grown-ups.

KEEPING THE ENTREPRENEURIAL MINDSET ALIVE

The most outstanding talent of humanity is adaptability. When the chips are down and adversity sets in, we have a natural ability to adapt and prevail. But our brains are naturally hard-wired to resist change. We don't like it. In fact, part of our brain, the amygdala, interprets change as a threat and responds by releasing hormones that encourage 'fight or flight'. We prefer to be in our comfort zone.

However, the 'comfort zone' doesn't naturally come to mind when considering entrepreneurs. Instead, it's easy to picture the fanatical founder obsessed with a product, naturally innovative, constantly networking, and showing off their 'baby' to others. The start-up mindset is usually associated with irresistible energy and inspirational founders who consistently push boundaries to achieve their dream. When the start-up mindset is written about, it's often connected with a vibrant and innovative company ready to take on the world.

Now, think about a large corporate organisation. Does that same vibrancy spring to mind? Some incredibly well-run and highly profitable companies are out there, but large organisations tend to become more bureaucratic and complex and, therefore, slower to adapt. This is natural. As exciting as start-ups are, they are typically neither efficient nor profitable. Successfully scaling a business demands more governance and increasing formality to ensure the needs of shareholders are met. However, this so often comes at the expense of being able to innovate brilliantly.

For a company to break out of the inevitable decline of the typical business life cycle, meaningful innovation is essential. The phoenix may rise from the ashes, but the phoenix is a myth. To unlock the secret of sustainable growth, the organisation must keep the innovation muscle alive. So, how do we do this in practice?

The typical image of the start-up founder does not sit comfortably within most large organisations. Entrepreneurs mix with bureaucracy as well as oil mixes with water. Yet, there is a way of keeping the flame of innovation burning brightly. Continuing to find a way to empower fanatical founders within a large organisation can be the secret to growth. Organisations of all shapes and sizes must be efficient and innovative for genuinely sustainable development. They must become ambidextrous. There are people who can cut through the organisation's red tape and maintain the entrepreneurial spirit. Phil Knight and Steve Jobs are probably the most pointed to.

DEMYSTIFYING THE MYSTERIES OF START-UP INNOVATION

Start-ups are naturally innovative. They have to be. It is their *raison d'être*. By its very definition, a start-up is starting something new. If it doesn't create a successful product or service, it will cease trading, or never get off the ground.

History tends to be written by the victors, so it's no surprise that the most successful start-ups dominate the column inches devoted to entrepreneurship. There are many true stories of maverick founders overcoming all odds with inspiring grit and determination. But there are also many untold stories of entrepreneurs calling it a day and failing to find the fabled 'product-market fit'. There are many valuable lessons to be learned from both.

So, what characterises successful entrepreneurs? Perhaps most importantly, the founders are on a mission, single-mindedly running at a goal and unerringly focused on developing their venture. Founders are also agile, making quick decisions and pivoting where needed. There are no rules to follow, nor is there anything to lose.

A start-up business is often a highly charged, highly flexible environment. When there are no established processes and no established cost base, the founder can direct the company in a different direction without notice and without cost. There is, after all, no one to tell them 'no'. There is no legal team offering counsel for every thought, no procurement department advocating for the approved providers. There is no risk function to highlight potential downsides and adverse consequences of decision-making. Speed, agility and single-minded determination are the most potent weapons for a small business.

BIG COMPANIES STRUGGLE TO CREATE

A start-up is a fast-paced environment, but paradoxically, it can also be a more patient one. What success looks like to a start-up is very different from that of an established business. The success criteria for transformational innovation within a large organisation are often way too ambitious. The timelines are unrealistic, and the sales targets are unachievable.

Back in 2005, I was asked to work with a global drinks company on an innovation review. The focus was on why its new product launches were failing. As well as its core behemoth product, it released a handful of other products, none of which you'd likely remember. For the review, I spoke to twenty-three executives and consulted seemingly endless internal and external documents and sources. The main conclusions can be bucketed into five fundamental failings. You may recognise some from your organisations.

UNREALISTIC EXPECTATIONS
Expectations were set too high. From the initial forecast to the subsequent marketing plans, the leadership team were

presented prospects that were just too ambitious. There was no room for error or delay.

LAST MINUTE COMPROMISES

Innovative concepts were not given the space to breathe in their purest form. Senior leadership imposed alterations to the foundation blocks of the idea very late in the day. Pricing was changed from the early plans, primarily driven by pressure for profit.

PERSONALITY TRUMPING DATA

Personalities and personal judgement outweighed the proposed process and success criteria. The launches ended up being rushed, and some key elements were untested. The instincts of senior leaders were, surprisingly (!?), not always right. In some cases, data also trumps courage.

LACK OF POST-LAUNCH ATTENTION

So much focus was put on getting ready for launch, and so little time was given to post-launch reviews and actions. Although these launches were niche, they were largely forgotten as soon as they were put into the market.

LACK OF PATIENCE

Overall, these projects didn't receive sufficient continued support to give them a chance to succeed, and were loaded with unrealistic expectations. One executive surmised that *'the system has little or no patience for new brands... unless they are successful in two to three months, they are dead.'* Another: *'If the system was asked to launch [the core product] today, it would fail.'*

What astonished me most was how well these launches had performed when compared to other new launches in the category. The problem was that they were oversold and given too much distribution from the beginning (before the sales run rate grew). Then, the marketing was pulled before it could influence purchase behaviour.

Another executive reflected: *'We have a choice. Either we*

should create a nursery to enable new brands to grow into scale,
create products with instant scale, or go into acquisition mode.'

As the last quote identified, they needed an innovation nursery, patience and a healthy dose of FORGE thinking!

BUT START-UPS
STRUGGLE TO SCALE

Big companies might struggle to create, but start-ups struggle to scale. The UK is a nation of small businesses. More than 5.5 million businesses are in the UK, but 4.1 million have no employees. Only 8,000 firms have more than 250 employees. Scaling from a start-up is hard.

Irene Graham is the CEO of the ScaleUp Institute, an organisation dedicated to ensuring that the UK is the best place in the world to start and scale a business. The organisation was started after a 2013 study demonstrated that while the UK was third in the world for starting a business, it was thirteenth in the world for scaling them up.

Irene told me, "We found several advantages that the UK perhaps didn't have; which the other countries that were ahead of us did. One was the depth of capital across the UK in terms of funding for a scale-up journey, whether that be institutional capital or sovereign wealth funds. The other was just the lack of long-term vision and agencies that could focus on the scale-up economy.

"Other challenges for our scale-up CEOs were access to talent, access to markets, access to funding and growth capital, access to space to grow, and also developing their leadership team.'

Irene also went on to talk about the importance of local ecosystems and of those growing pains – implementing procedures and processes while staying innovative. You'll find her well-earned tips in this book.

But it's worth looking at why start-ups struggle to scale. If you work within a larger business, it might help you to see what your unfair advantage really is. There are clear and common reasons start-ups struggle to scale:

TALENT AND SKILLS

Retaining talent and finding good people with relevant skills and experience is a constant challenge as companies grow. It's often cited as the most painful part of expanding a business. Employing the wrong people can have a significant negative impact on the company.

LEADERSHIP

Scaling a business is challenging and requires changes that aren't easy for entrepreneurs to make. A born entrepreneur isn't necessarily a born leader of a scaling business.

FINANCE

I'm yet to meet a start-up entrepreneur who wouldn't take the financial advantages a big business could provide, but only if they came without strings attached. Cash flow is king, and start-ups in a pre-launch phase have very little. Raising finance can become a full-time job.

NETWORKS AND CONNECTIONS

The right connections need to be nurtured, whether by a small business or a large organisation. These can help any new venture navigate the labyrinth of finding genuinely useful support and provide access to the markets required to fuel scaling.

But some start-ups do scale, grow and turn into large businesses. Then, something happens to them that could ultimately kill them. Let's delve into the realms of becoming big.

WHY GROWING COMPANIES LOSE THE ENTREPRENEURIAL MINDSET

A business is like a living organism, constantly growing, with different parts moving at different speeds. This evolution brings challenges. The culture shifts, the structure calcifies, and resource allocation challenges emerge. It's a necessary part of growing up; processes need to be more efficient, but – and here's the paradox again – the very reasons that led it to be successful in the first place, the agility and environment to be innovative, are squeezed out. Here's how a company typically changes as it grows:

SLOWER DECISION-MAKING

No longer is it one or two founders making a decision; different stakeholders and layers of approval are involved; and new functions, including legal and procurement 'support', are to be considered. As more people are involved, businesses typically develop more layers of management and increasingly formal processes that need to be navigated to get decisions approved. This increased bureaucracy slows down decision-making. It's inefficient and ineffective.

THE SPEED OF EXECUTION DECREASES

As the organisation becomes more extensive and complex, it requires more time, effort and people to successfully execute change, leading to a loss of agility. Everything is a little slower. Implementing change and executing it becomes slower. The value proposition development, the rate of trialling new products, and the measurement are all slowing down. The start-up's essential advantage is lost. It's also inefficient and slow.

REDUCED APPETITE FOR RISK

Now that the business is growing, has employees, and has a customer base, it has something to lose. Often, it develops a belief that more success will follow if it just keeps doing what it's doing. A company will naturally want to protect its position in the market and its employees. This, in turn, sows the seeds of risk aversion. There will be no jumping at an opportunity on a whim. There is a reduced appetite for change; there is something to lose.

SHORT-TERMISM CREEPS IN

As more traditional business planning develops, annual budgets and quarterly targets become more important. This can lead to a short-term financial focus, often to the detriment of activities requiring longer timescales, namely innovation. New projects require approval within the annual financial cycle. Agile, this is not.

LESS FOCUSED ACCOUNTABILITY

Companies naturally divide when they grow. Departments develop across functions or territory. In a divided company, however, your people feel further from the decision-making. This can lead to a reduction in accountability. No longer is everyone fully embedded in the mission. And even those in high-level roles often struggle to see the big picture. This can lead to disengagement if sufficient focus isn't nurtured.

SILOED THINKING

The organisation becomes siloed as those different departments, functions and, ultimately, divisions develop. Without this constant interaction, there is little cross-pollination of ideas. Communication suffers.

RESOURCE COMPETITION

There's a spreadsheet somewhere with a number on it, and that's the budget. How that gets divided up is a critical business decision. But now there is competition for it. How much goes into the product? Customer services need to raise their game, and the marketing department passionately believes a TV campaign is the way to gain more customers. Who gets that resource is a difficult and complex decision. Each department's innovation must be fully funded. Often, it is not.

WHAT HAPPENS TO A COMPANY WHEN THERE ARE GROWING PAINS

Growth leads to the organisation becoming slower, safer and siloed. This is not the most conducive environment for new ideas to take hold. Efficient? Yes. Profitable? Yes. The makings of a successful business. Well, no. Not unless you ensure that innovation can also flourish. It's right at this stage – not a moment longer – when we need to recognise what might have been lost in the scaling process.

Gone are speed, agility, risk-taking, and, if we're not incredibly careful, the founder mindset, entrepreneurial focus and startling distinctiveness that made the original product so compelling. This book addresses the challenge – a challenge that, if not articulated successfully, will lead to the inevitable decline in the business.

Executives usually recognise this. But even if they do, the typical response just doesn't work. Over the following five chapters, I'm giving you the toolkit to ensure that the Focus, the Originality, the Results, the Growth and the Ecosystem are primed for success. It's a proven dynamic approach, but first, it's worth looking at the typical response from an organisation that has recognised the need for innovation. See if your organisation has fallen into any of these traps.

HOW DO ORGANISATIONS TRY TO OVERCOME GROWING PAINS?

Faced with these challenges of scaling, executives need to act. Fast. Yet, sometimes, it's difficult to see the true picture. Everyone typically agrees that 'innovation' is essential. Everyone typically agrees that the organisation needs to become more 'agile'. Very few have been in a similar situation before, nor with a practical toolkit for how to act. Very few can lean on their entrepreneurial experiences to keep the innovation flame burning bright. So what do they do? They follow 'best practice'. Or consultants. Either way, below are some typical responses and, of course, a big 'but'. Traditional wisdom has repeatedly proven to break down in a world of increasing uncertainty.

TOP-DOWN MANDATE

A meeting will be called, and a memo will be disseminated asking managers for growth. There is a clear top-down mandate for innovation. An increase in R&D spending may be possible. All very good then.

THE BIG 'BUT'

A mandate isn't enough. As we'll discover in the Focus chapter, we must spend a long time defining the problem we want to address (spoiler alert: we don't want to fall in love with a solution that doesn't address a problem). Any mandate that is passed down is often poorly defined: 'We need to make more money.' Innovation is a mindset, and that needs to come from the top. But too often, with the mandate comes constraints that are too tight and expectations that are too high. In some cases I've seen, bonus targets for executives are linked to the performance and cadence of an innovation project. This is not the right environment for innovation. We're not advocating for no accountability, but give us a chance to think freely. Almost always, the best ideas come from those closest to the problem.

THE STAGE-GATE PROCESS

Most larger organisations take on the idea of an innovation pipeline. They shoot the new initiatives through a stage-gate process, tracking the progression of ideas into, hopefully, successful outcomes. The stage-gate process forces a series of 'go' or 'no go' decisions along the way. It provides prompts to ask every question an innovation needs. It also gives a budgetary mechanism. If product X makes it to the next stage, it unlocks resources. It's tidy, it's neat.

Internal barriers. Speed and agility are among a start-up's most significant advantages. The stage-gate process, to use an adjacent metaphor, closes barriers at every stage. The internal preparation required to pass through each one reduces the time for actual market validation. The stage-gate pipeline looks less like a funnel and more like parallel tracks leaving a train station. Each product is on its own, with its barriers, red signals and 'leaves on the line'.

Lack of post-launch feedback. Phew, we made it. We can all breathe a sigh of relief as our product is finally launched to market and turn to the next thing. After all, the stage-gate process asked all the right questions, right? What is often lacking here are the post-launch questions. Gathering our learnings is perhaps one of the most important elements, but it so frequently gets lost in pursuit of the next shiny thing.

MAKE INNOVATION PART OF EVERYONE'S ROLE

This is a lovely idea. It will be 'empowering'. Innovation absolutely should be part of everyone's job – the constant incremental improvement of the employees' sphere of influence is what makes businesses move and improve and, let's be honest, makes work fulfilling. However, this approach errs on the side of caution, it is incremental change to the core proposition. Often, it falls to the marketing or product teams for innovative ideas to be pushed through.

THE BIG 'BUT'

Does anyone have time for 'innovation' when managing a warehouse, trying to get a campaign live, making a product work, and raising the NPS score? Day-to-day jobs just don't allow enough space for creative thinking, no matter how much the leadership team is 'listening'.

I believe it can and should be part of everyone's job, but it will usually be related to 'core' innovation, the optimising of a product that is already in existence and has a market. Innovation is incremental and manageable. If something is broken or not working as efficiently as it can, no matter which department you're in, you'll look for a solution.

Trickier is 'Adjacent' innovation, the type of venture that sees a business expand into a 'new to the company' business. Perhaps it is spirits for a beer company or batteries for a car manufacturer. It takes more innovative thinking and, moreover, a mindset that allows it the space to develop and launch.

The next level of innovation is 'Transformational', and is the hardest of all. It involves creating products for markets that don't exist yet.

INNOVATION LABS

Nothing screams 'corporate cool' like an innovation lab. A 'skunk works' even. Otherwise known as a central innovation team, this is the team that everyone wants to be on. They imagine an environment of walks and talks in the park, hackathons, and trips to other (non-competing) companies. Get some mavericks in a room. Lean into Agile. Lots of blue sky. These people cannot be in the same building as the corporate ones. They are building the future.

THE BIG 'BUT'

Beyond ignoring the awkwardness of telling friends at a dinner party you're on the 'disruption' team, several issues must be overcome when building a central innovation team. A typical phenomenon in a business is for the best people to be given the most prominent roles. The size of accountability matters, certainly when it comes to promotions. Innovation, by definition, starts small. So does that mean that only the second-tier players should apply?

However, these 'innovation' teams rarely work as planned. Yes, there will be good intentions and genuine effort, but a company's rigorous processes often stifle innovation. Fast-paced decision-making just can't happen without considerable autonomy.

CORPORATE VENTURE CAPITAL

We can do everything a VC can, but we'll also bring our 'unfair advantage' to the table. Start-ups will be beating down our door, desperate to work with us. Not only is this a clever use of our capital, but it will also help us gain market insights and access to the latest industry innovations.

THE BIG 'BUT'

Corporate venture capital (CVC) usually attempts to emulate how pure venture capital (VC) operates, but it is susceptible to many of the same issues as developing an innovation lab. One is the general misalignment of the CVC's goals with those of the start-up. VCs tend to be more patient with their capital.

There are other complications, too. Developing an exit strategy for CVC investments is notoriously complex, even if that is transferring CVC innovation back to the mothership. And it's unlikely the organisation has the in-house skills to manage a venture capital portfolio. This means it needs to attract talent from the VC world... and at great expense. None of this helps build the innovation muscle within the team.

MULTIPLE MINDSETS NEEDED

WE'VE EXAMINED SOME OF THE characteristics that make start-ups innovative and why large companies struggle to foster an environment for innovation. Here, I want to say that we're looking for more radical innovation, the type that answers some of the questions posed in chapter one.

We know that early-stage ventures require an entrepreneurial mindset, one characterised by grit, determination and resilience in the face of failure. One that is single-minded in the pursuit of something tremendous and selfish in getting the outcome. We want a growth mindset over a return on investment. We need efficiency *and* innovation. And we never want to downgrade our ambition. All this is what often makes start-ups successful.

In the second half of this book we're going to make that path clear with a simple, effective, and memorable framework, FORGE. For now, let's take the example of a huge corporation that already blends mindsets well, starting with Procter & Gamble. Procter & Gamble has a proud history since 1837 and is one of the longest-serving members of the New York Stock Exchange (NYSE). Today, it generates revenues of over $82 billion and has 107,000 global employees. Starting as a soap and candle business, it has continually innovated and extended its product lines and now has more than 20 'billion-dollar brands'. One of the key reasons for this is its innovation strategy. It opened its first research and development (R&D) lab in 1890. That's not a typo. More than 135 years ago, it understood the need for rapid and protected innovation. Then, in 2000, CEO A.G. Lafley also understood that it couldn't maintain its 'invent it ourselves' approach and developed a 'connect and develop' initiative, collaborating with suppliers, scientists, universities, entrepreneurs and even competitors on products that P&G can improve, scale and market. This structure allows P&G to focus on incremental innovation within its established product lines while also exploring new growth opportunities through external collaborations and partnerships. This dual focus has enabled P&G to maintain leadership in the consumer goods sector by continuously evolving its product offerings.

The question, therefore, becomes: How do we blend the entrepreneur's mindset with an established business's clear advantages and resources? The entrepreneur gazing into the future could only dream of the resources that large companies enjoy. At the same time, the corporate leader ponders, misty-eyed behind them, wishing that they or at least someone in the organisation had the freedom of a start-up. FORGE helps make that path clear.

To consider the multiple mindsets needed, I've found it helpful to divide the stages of innovation ventures – the current status the venture is on – into three: Ignite, Incubate and Integrate/Independence. These three sections offer a clear framework for what is required at each stage.

STAGE ONE: IGNITE
EMPOWERING 'ENTREPRENEURS WITHIN'

We're holding up a big signpost that reads: 'Innovation begins here'. It's the ignition stage of our business life cycle. And you are the entrepreneur within. Let's remind ourselves who that is. I particularly like the definition from Steve Glaveski: 'An entrepreneur challenges the status quo and attempts to solve problems and create value by taking something fundamentally new, but fraught with uncertainty and risk, to the world.'

As the innovator-in-chief, the entrepreneur within, the

founder in an organisation, perhaps after a buyout, or asked to lead a new product, you may not have been rewarded in an organisation that places a higher value on predictability and mitigating risk. But we need to ensure the best people become innovation leaders. These are the intrapreneurs who will challenge that status quo, solve a big problem and create value, who will excel in the ambiguity of innovation. Often, the 'best' people are given the big jobs, the division with the most significant turnover, or a flagship product; however, they could be better suited to innovation, new products, and those with risk.

The intrapreneur or founder within a business requires many of the same characteristics as an entrepreneur, but there are nuanced differences. You are acting as an entrepreneur but within the constraints (and with the advantages) of a large business. The ideal entrepreneur within an organisation needs to be:

» A champion. Is passionate about the problem – maybe because of personal experience – and is a strong advocate for the vision.

» Charismatic. Has strong communication and sales skills, essential to attracting people. Building relationships is beneficial for accessing resources within the organisation.

» Committed. Believes in the plan and just gets stuff done. Has the grit and staying power needed to nurture a new venture through good and bad times. Persistence to keep going when things are tough; has the ability to bounce back from adversity. Keeps the idea alive.

» Curious. Is particularly deft at avoiding herd mentality, is open-minded and adaptable. Constantly questioning how and why things are done. Will always be hunting for better solutions.

» Courageous. Embraces calculated risk-taking and accepts ambiguity. Is eager to make the decisions that could expand the business, but is accountable for them.

» Commercial. Focused on the critical few priorities – the important rather than the seemingly urgent – not distracted from the core mission. Finds a way to work within the organisation's commercial strategy and systems.

In the same way that an entrepreneur takes on mentorship, it's vital that these intrapreneurs are supported by coaching and by people who have done something similar before. It doesn't matter whether this is internal or external. It does matter, however, that this mentoring is seen as part of the intrapreneurial deal and not an additional cost to be allocated to the new venture's P&L.

We need to give them space, the freedom to cut through red tape, and the mandate to make mistakes. These entrepreneurs within need protection from the very top of the organisation to ensure they are truly empowered. The next step takes this further.

STAGE TWO: INCUBATE
BALANCING THE FOUNDING TEAM

Once a new idea gets initial traction, when it's launched, when we've sold some widgets, when we've developed an audience, it's time to expand the team from an intrapreneur to a balanced founding team. This is the Blaze phase of our business life cycle, the moment when we reach product-market fit.[5]

The most important concept here is to free up the entrepreneur within to obsess about product-market fit. Finding a 'co-founder' specifically within the role of internal Chief Operating Officer (COO) makes this possible. They navigate internal bureaucracy and dynamics, shielding the founder against the prying eyes of leadership. The internal ecosystem around the new venture assists the business – there are skills, knowledge and finance if required – but the COO is the gatekeeper. But nor can a fledgling venture be overwhelmed with 'help'; it needs to be free of the restrictive processes of a large organisation and be empowered.

TOOLS AND THINKING

Once the core duo of the CEO and the COO is established, the team will grow further as appropriate, with new talent typically leading sales, marketing, administration and technical delivery. But at all times, this founding team must maintain the start-up mindset. They require the right tools and thinking to successfully operate within a large organisation. The tools they need to survive and adapt in a very uncertain environment differ significantly from those in a relatively stable and established business. It's roll-your-sleeves-up time for everyone.

To be a successful innovator, you must take a deep-thinking approach to a problem and explore it in many different ways. This differs from shallowly discussing several issues that managing a project in the corporate world requires. Access to knowledge and experience, especially outside the organisation, is essential to help with your thought processes.

URGENT VS IMPORTANT: RUTHLESS FOCUS

Another nuanced difference for an organisation's founding team is to be clear about the most critical outcomes. You need to know what you're aiming for and then work backwards to work out what you need to achieve this. Be ruthless about what you need to be true about your situation in 90 days. It will be tough to accomplish if you don't know what you're aiming for. It's also the time to start considering a dedicated growth board. We'll discuss this further in, yep, Growth.

STAGE THREE:
INTEGRATE OR INDEPENDENCE
*READYING TO RETURN TO THE MOTHERSHIP
(OR NOT)*

The long-term ambition is often for the innovation venture to be passed back to the core business, the mothership. If you're plotting this on the business life cycle diagram, then it is the point after Blaze and at the start of Combustion.

The structure of the founding team was set up to help this shift back; for example, having a COO who deals with the processes and politics of the mothership allows the rest of the team to get on with doing what they do best.

However, before it's fully integrated, the venture first needs to prove that it could continue to thrive within a corporate environment. For this to happen, there needs to be a clear definition of roles and responsibilities, a knowledge transfer plan, and a clear direction for how the venture will integrate with existing budgets and targets, especially how to integrate the cost base.

It also needs to be comfortable with the functional divisions it will ultimately be integrated into. In the beginning, the team is working closely, often across functions. However, when being beamed into the mothership, the activities – whether marketing or logistics, supply or product – must be mapped into the relevant departments. If the best outcome for an innovation venture becomes independence, then it will need to function as a standalone business from the moment that decision is taken.

BECOMING AMBIDEXTROUS

To reiterate, becoming ambidextrous means being efficient *and* innovative. The rest of this book is dedicated to explaining exactly how to do that. It sets the entrepreneurial mindset, that free-thinking creativity, that innovation muscle, the fast-moving spirit of a start-up and balances it against the rigour and necessary considerations of a large-scale business. It will give you guidance for creating an innovative environment, for ensuring you focus on the right problem, for measuring only the metrics that matter, for achieving growth in a sustainable and manageable way, and for making the most of the networks within and outside of the organisation. I've called my methodology for achieving innovation and efficiency FORGE. It stands for Focus, Originality, Results, Growth and Ecosystem.

So let's get focused first.

PART 2

FOCUS

ORIGINALITY

RESULTS

APO · SUMMICRON · M 1:2/50 ASPH

GROWTH

ECOSYSTEM

THE FORGE
METHODOLOGY

FORGING INNOVATION

PART ONE OF THE BOOK DEMONSTRATED *why* innovation is essential for long-term business success. Now, we move into the FORGE methodology. This is the 'how-to'. The design for our FORGE lettering is no coincidence: I see the methodology like a series of pipes, all interconnected but with innovation flowing throughout.

Each of the following chapters that make up the FORGE methodology – **Focus**, **Originality**, **Results**, **Growth** and **Ecosystem** – are interconnected elements. While there is a logical order to them, I'm not calling them steps because the relevancy is directly related to where you are in your innovation journey.

Within each of the next five chapters, you'll find a range of tools to help you innovate and scale. I've distilled decades of knowledge and experience, and have incorporated advice from interviews with pioneers from some of the world's most innovative companies, including Apple, Nike and Sony. I've spoken to business leaders and organisational gurus. I've heard the tales from the frontline of innovation, and where they've tripped up or found unexpected success. These learnings are all within the next chapters.

I've also been directly involved with hundreds of innovation projects. I've seen wild successes and painful (oh so painful) failures. I've launched products from scratch and moved products to greater heights. I've worked with dozens of organisations too, from major banks to universities, vast corporations to government-run hubs. I've had the opportunity to see first-hand why some innovations succeed and some fail.

I started then to organise my experiences to understand why some things succeeded and others failed. What became very clear is that it wasn't all about the product or service. There were a huge number of factors at play. And I started to group them. When things do go wrong, it's typically because at least one of the FORGE elements – outlined below – is missing.

INTRODUCING FORGE

All these experiences inspired me to codify the elements needed to lead innovation. Through my experience and talking to intrapreneurs and entrepreneurs who number in the hundreds, I found that the same five problem areas kept coming up.

FOCUS

We may have a great product, but is it actually solving a genuine problem for the audience? I've seen many ideas fall by the wayside because they don't answer a problem. Focus is about finding the problem first and discarding anything else. There are also great innovations that just don't fit with the company's ethos and, therefore, die a slow death, underloved and under-resourced. Focus is about where to shine the light for future innovation. The problem also must sync with your purpose, your capabilities and the market trends. When they are, there's a much greater chance of success. There is a labyrinth of routes to head down; this is about finding the right path and embarking on your quest.

ORIGINALITY

Once you've found your problem, Originality is about applying your creative techniques to find initiatives worthy of attention. Original thinking does not require magic stardust; not every idea needs to be sparklingly original, but we need a creative proposition that stands out. To do so, we need to remove the shackles of existing thought patterns ('we've tried that', 'they've tried that', 'it won't work'). Originality gives a toolkit to get the best out of any team and teaches to hone them into the solutions to be tested. Genuine innovation has no experts. This chapter offers ways to do precisely that.

RESULTS

This chapter is about validating the concepts quickly, in the market, not the boardroom, and then rapidly adapting to gain traction or failing speedily and with little cost. Far too many innovations get caught up in meeting rooms and left lingering on unread PowerPoint presentations, within focus meeting notes or on spreadsheets. Most importantly, this chapter is about measuring the right things and cutting out the noise. Here, we scrutinise the lead indicators of Desirability, Viability and Feasibility to increase learning velocity. We're testing whether people want to buy it, whether we can make money from it, and whether we can fulfil it. I've said before, but there's never been a better time to test a product at lightning speed and cheaply.

GROWTH

Once we've got an idea that has had some traction, we turn our attention to Growth. How do we move from the start-up mode to rapidly scaling without losing momentum? This is the time to place the big bets, but recognise that innovation is essential for scaling and ensuring continuous success. Common problems in large organisations include ventures not getting the attention they deserve, funding drying up, or not having a passionate founder to continue pushing, pushing and pushing. What got you so far is unlikely to be the same combination of elements to scale.

ECOSYSTEM

From the very outset, you need great people and support around you, whether within a large business or just starting a new venture. This was a key learning for me. I've always been a prolific networker, but I've really dug into what environment is required for a network that benefits everyone in it. Ecosystem is about creating the environment for sustainable success, harnessing the wider community to provide fuel for the business, and opening up a pipeline for future growth. This means getting the best talent and skills, specialist knowledge, finance and networks.

The positive news is that innovation (despite the fact that one of my tools is actually labelled 'ROCKET') is not rocket science. It's about incremental changes, fostering a mindset and creating an environment, one step at a time.

HOW TO USE FORGE

The elements within FORGE are designed to help you diagnose problems and discover where things should be strengthened. I understand that many readers of this book will find themselves at the Results stage or even Growth. By all means, jump right into those chapters. You need to face up to the immediate challenges, and the book is designed to allow you to do that.

Each chapter is loaded with tools – these are models, some with pleasing acronyms, that will save you time. Every part of the process, from finding the problem to solve to repositioning a successful venture back into the main organisation, has been considered, researched and tested.

Innovation is a skill that can be taught and trained; it can be developed like a muscle. FORGE is your training plan, offering structure to become a better innovator. A framework that also helps you identify gaps and diagnose where things may be going wrong.

Great innovation has the power to transform business growth while making a meaningful difference in the world. That's why we do what we do, and that's why you're reading this book. My hope is that the FORGE methodology will provide you with the tools to boost innovation in your company. The power of innovation, of progress, is in your hands. Let's get to it...

FOCUS

WHY FOCUS MATTERS

'If you chase two rabbits,
you catch no rabbits.'
LATIN PROVERB

'If you chase a hare by mistake,
you also get no rabbits.'
AUTHOR'S ATTEMPT AT HUMOUR

THE ART OF CHASING RABBITS

This chapter is all about chasing the right rabbit. It's about picking one and focusing on that and nothing else. It's about picking the right problem (not the solution) to focus on. The chasing of too many ideas or the wrong ideas becomes a stumbling block over which companies, large and small, fall foul again and again. It's the battle against trying to do too much. As Herbert Bayard Swope said, "I can't give you a sure-fire formula for success, but I can give you a formula for failure: try to please everybody."

Whatever the reason for embarking on your innovation journey, let's recognise the value of getting started. Effective innovation – that is, innovation that actually changes behaviour and meets the ambitions set for it – requires thoughtful targeting and rigour.

No matter whether you are leading complex change programmes in big corporations, starting a new venture by yourself, supporting others in their innovation endeavours or simply looking for ways to fuel future growth, there are some common principles which will help ensure you find the focus and lead to greater returns.

SPEED DOES NOT EQUAL VELOCITY

Given the pace of change around us and the extent to which businesses of all types must continuously adapt, it's no surprise that speed is often seen as a driving force behind new initiatives and decisions. Moving fast can be important.

But just as in physics, there's a distinction between speed and velocity. Speed is the rate at which an object is moving along a path, while velocity is the rate of an object's movement in a given direction. The key word to note here is 'direction'.

Focus provides the compass to guide us through the landscape of possibilities and help us navigate to the ideas that could make the difference.

Let's be honest: Focus can take a bit of time. It requires slowing down, and taking a step back before being able to stride forward, but that clear direction makes the difference between something moving fast (speed) and something moving with purpose (velocity).

So, what obstacles prevent us from achieving Focus and reaching the desired velocity? There are many ways to lose focus, but let's run through some of the most common stumbling blocks.

RECOGNISING THE RABBIT HOLES

It is precisely because Focus requires something more than just 'getting on with it' that it's all too easy to skip this stage and bulldoze forward in the pursuit of quicker returns. Or, more dangerous, to believe that you're applying Focus but actually only paying lip service to it.

So, typically, businesses (forgive the overegging of the rabbit-chasing metaphor here) fall down a number of common rabbit holes as they strive to innovate at speed but without direction (velocity).

1. THE SCATTERGUN APPROACH
The name makes it clear. In this scenario, businesses conjure up a myriad of possible ideas and fire them off to see which ones stick. I've spoken to so many businesses – small and large – and asked them to succinctly articulate the problem they are focused on and to define where the growth is going

to be coming from, and I've had so many varied answers. All have tried to articulate it; very few have been able to articulate it succinctly.

This is the feeling that all progress is good progress. This is the myth that speed equals velocity. The ones that can clearly demonstrate at least the direction they are heading are the ones that typically have a track record of success.

One theme that comes up alarmingly regularly is that businesses see so many opportunities or are working on so many different projects that there are never enough resources (or breathing space) for one thing to become great. Those rabbits are breeding again. Not being able to focus clearly on the 'new' is one of the single biggest reasons that businesses aren't able to reinvent themselves or to scale.

Of course, companies can go to market with the best of the bunch or even launch multiple products into the market. Together, these might indeed add up to a sizeable scale of 'innovation-led growth' but are individually small-scale and, therefore, are likely to have limited lifespans. At some point, complexity will lead to a cull.

This is frequently the case in well-established Fast-Moving Consumer Goods (FMCG) categories, where driving meaningful behaviour change is difficult and where the value of novelty is relatively high.

A quick look at the UK confectionery category reveals the problem with this approach. Seven of top ten 'singles' products are the same today as they were a decade ago (and not wildly different from those five decades ago). It demonstrates just how little innovation has cut through or has been truly innovative enough to do so. This is not an industry that is breaking through to new audiences, despite an enormous number of new ways of covering things in cheap chocolate.

2. FALLING IN LOVE WITH THE SOLUTION

I see this a lot. There's this shiny new thing. An amazing proprietary technology or product or service or idea that's just waiting to shine. And why wouldn't it? After all, the

CEO's spouse adores it. Your friend is already telling their friends, and your child loves it! It's a no-brainer. Get it moving. And given the set-up here, you'll see I'm about to put the brakes on.

The myth here is that we convince ourselves that we have the best solution. We now just need to find the customers who will also realise how wonderful our solution is.

Of course, there is a case for sweating the existing assets. This can be enormously valuable for large corporations with established manufacturing and patents. However, there is an equally huge risk of falling in love with a solution that doesn't have a problem big enough or valuable enough to be worth solving.

Let's talk peas. Now, you may have cutting-edge freezing technology that enables every frozen pea to be of superior quality. But who eats a plate of peas? Consumers instead are looking for full-plate solutions: tastier, healthier meals, of which the humble pea plays just a small part. Plus, pea-freezing technology is already pretty good. True innovation is about consumer needs. Innovation needs to be problem-led, not solution-led.

3. NODDING TO THE NOW

With the absence of a crystal ball, it is notoriously tricky to predict future consumer needs. Who, after all, in 2019, could possibly have predicted the cataclysmic change about to be wrought on global purchase and consumption patterns? But keeping the current category blinkers on is a surefire way to kill ideas before they've had a chance.

The myth here is that the world isn't changing. That new technologies or changes in consumer behaviour won't disrupt. That something unexpected won't happen.

Adaptation, tweaking and continuous iteration are fine for incremental innovation, but for anything more disruptive, we must consider future potential rather than current opportunity, based on the current market and consumer-shopper behaviour. Being too focused on the present may cause you to miss viable opportunities.

Like all methodologies and models, there will always be an exception to the rule. There will always be occasions when a speedy piece of innovation has its place, for example, to capitalise on a particular consumer moment, maximise potential with excess manufacturing capacity, or on specific retailer demands. But, in general, these will be short-term, often self-limiting opportunities rather than the big innovations on which the future is built. As Wayne Gretzky famously answered, 'I skate to where the puck will be, not where it's been.'

4. ASSUMING WE HAVE FOCUS (WHEN WE DON'T)

It's all too easy for a business to assume there is a clear focus on innovation efforts when there isn't. Most businesses will say they have an 'innovation strategy', few will be able to articulate it succinctly, and – we're getting to the real essence of the problem – even fewer will allocate appropriate resources.

There is an admittedly understandable propensity to allocate resources to the core business. It delivers the financial targets (at least in the near term). It's exceptionally hard for businesses to dedicate those resources to an often less-defined problem outside of that core. The thinking is that this might adversely risk those all-important targets, but this may give away the long-term prize.

5. STRETCHING BEYOND YOUR LIMITS

Understanding your purpose, brand and business identity is a critical part of Focus. You need to stay true to who you are and what your business does. Avoid leaping into spaces that might be right for your audience but not necessarily right for you. Just because you can, doesn't mean that you should.

The myth here is that consumers already think so highly of your brand that it can naturally stretch to all other aspects of their lives. It can be hard to ignore a new opportunity, but understanding that a brand – or business – can't be everything to everyone is an essential element of Focus. This is a point well understood by Google, which applies a 'Googl-ey' challenge to any idea. They ask themselves 'would Google do this?'

Unsurprisingly, this is where mergers and acquisitions often occur. Recognising that brand expansion, even into adjacent categories, isn't always a natural fit is a significant driver in businesses acquiring new brands that can support their ambitions. A clear example is The Coca-Cola Company's acquisition of Innocent Drinks.

Of course, this challenge presupposes that the business or brand has a clear sense of self in the first place. If not, there's a whole step back to go through before we even get to the opportunity focus for growth.

If any of these rabbit holes sounds familiar, read on. By the end of this chapter, I'm sure you'll have a very clear idea of which rabbit to chase... and I promise not to talk about rabbits anymore.

STEPPING BACK
TO LEAP FORWARDS

*'Innovation comes from
saying no to a thousand things.'*
STEVE JOBS

HUMANS ARE BUILT TO CHANGE AND EVOLVE.
Adaptability is one of mankind's greatest assets. But
successful adaptation has a reason.

Business is no different. Change is not beneficial for
its own sake; there must be a reason. Change expends
resources, requires decisions, and involves risk; it can't
happen lightly and rarely succeeds by chance.

Being able to articulate your innovation 'why' is the
fundamental first step; it's the north star to help guide
you through uncharted territory, keep you fixed on the
destination and bring everyone on the journey together.
Finding your 'why' defines what your innovation is intended
to achieve. Fall in love with your problem.

For entrepreneurs, this may well be as personal as
much as commercial. It could be the desire to unlock a
completely different way of life from what they've had
before, or it could be much bigger and more far-reaching,
such as a belief in the need to turn the tide on
environmental problems.

For established businesses, it's more likely to be
connected to their purpose, a need for growth, or to tackle
a very specific problem. The challenge is that we often
conflate multiple problems into one and expect innovation
to provide the answers. And when it ultimately cannot
deliver everything, it is deemed a failure.

Let's return to chocolate-covered things as an example.
In the 2010s, the 'better-for-you' launches in confectionery

were expected to deliver, and big. They combined the 'genuine' consumer need for healthier choices, demonstrated to external pressure groups the commitment to health, and were expected to deliver a compelling return on investment. It all added up to significant growth. What the innovations roundly ignored was whether anyone actually wanted healthier chocolate. Would you compromise on taste? The consumer need wasn't there.

A trap that some businesses fall into is believing the focus groups too much. There's little doubt that when asked if healthier chocolate seems like a good idea, the focus group respondent will say, 'Yes, healthy chocolate seems like a great idea.' But when you're exhaustedly staring at a Galaxy after an hour in Tesco with the kids, your mind is not thinking 'healthy'; it's thinking 'I deserve this'. The healthy alternative initiatives played a role in building credibility but should never have been expected to become 'the next big thing'. They weren't. How many 'healthy' chocolate bars do you have in the snack drawer? It's the 'chasing two rabbits' conundrum.

Finding the 'why' of innovation doesn't need to be complex, but it does require some frank unpicking of the current situation. You must continuously ask 'why' to fully define the single problem for which innovation may be the answer.

TALES, TRAPS AND TIPS
MARK SCOTT

Mark Scott is an investor, mentor, and speaker. He's the co-founder of Bella & Duke, a hugely successful raw pet food brand that was named one of the Sunday Times' Top 100 Fastest Growing Businesses.

ON FOCUS, FOCUS, FOCUS

I made the mistake of thinking that more means better, but that's certainly not the case. I remember from my sales background when we used to talk about a 100-watt light bulb that lights up a room, but if you focus it, it could burn through steel like a laser. That's one of my lessons in the many decades I've been building businesses: Focus, focus, focus.

ON CLARITY OF VISION

Successful people prove the model. They go out and make stuff happen, raise money, and attract great people. The biggest challenge for any entrepreneur is that if you don't have a big enough vision, you're not going to attract the best people. Just have clarity on what you want to achieve.

Where do you want to be in three years? It's such a simple thing. Say to yourself, "I want to be here in three years' time, so what do I need to do tomorrow to be there in three years' time."

My vision was to be the number one pet wellness business in the UK. I said, let's aim for £50 million valuation in three years. It took four years. We did it because we had that clarity of what we all wanted to do, and then we worked backwards. What do I need to do next year, next month, next week, tomorrow. So I knew, tomorrow, whether I was on target or not. It's as simple as that.

ON BALANCING PROGRESS WITH PERFECTION

Done is better than perfect. Just get out there and learn. Our product wasn't always right, but the valuable feedback we got from customers was immense. But we balanced this with: *'good enough is the enemy of greatness.'* They kind of contradict each other, but in some parts of our business, we just had to be the best. The food has to be made with the best ingredients we can get. However, for our marketing campaigns, we could try 10 different things and fail quickly. There's always one thing I say to a founder when I first meet them, I say, "No one cares whether you're successful or not, so you don't need to worry about messing up."

ON FOCUSING ON THE RIGHT METRICS

We ask: "If we spend a pound on marketing, how much money are we going to get back?" So if I spend a pound on marketing and within two years, I get three pounds back, any investor is going to ask: "How many pounds can I give you?" It's understanding those very basic metrics that make the big difference and clarity. We had a very clear path to profitability, and you've got to make sure you've got enough margin in order to do it.

ON BUILDING A COMMUNITY LED-ECOSYSTEM

Community is essential, especially with pets. Pet owners love to talk and share photographs. What I realised is that a lot of these brands have real followers, they have real fans, they have communities. But in a subscription, there is a thing called a death curve: when you reach a certain size, it becomes much more challenging to grow. It's really difficult. The only way to get around the death curve is to have a referral rate greater than one. People will stop other people in the park and ask them, "What do you feed your dog?" And proudly say, "I'm feeding my dog raw food; I'm feeding them Bella & Duke." That community is what helps grow a brand."

FINDING THE RIGHT PROBLEM FOR YOU

ONCE THERE IS A GENUINE COMMITMENT
to innovating, and you are clear on what it needs to deliver
to the business, the question becomes, 'where to go fishing?'
The natural reaction is to look at the business landscape,
find an apparent gap in the market, and off you go.
Inevitably, the answer is a little more nuanced than that, but
that doesn't mean it needs to be complex.

So, being practical, how do we break down what it
means to achieve focus? I find it helpful to remember this
as the 'Four Ps of Focus', namely: Purpose, Potential, Profit
and Prowess. We'll delve into them below, and then we'll
talk about the critical importance of timing.

THE FOUR PS (AND A T) OF FOCUS

There is a Japanese concept called *ikigai*,[6] which refers to the
belief that everyone has a reason to jump out of bed in the
morning. A sense of purpose, a reason for being. The term
combines two Japanese words: *iki*, meaning 'life' or 'alive',
and *gai*, meaning 'benefit' or 'worth'.

Although the origins of *ikigai* date back more than
1,000 years, a more contemporary interpretation has
developed in the business world. It suggests that the sweet
spot for entrepreneurial endeavours sits at the intersection
between what you love, what you are good at, what the
world needs and what people will pay for. It's this unique
blend which sets up the best chance of finding success.

I've built this thinking to help guide a more established business to focus on the right problem, and it's delightfully simple to apply. Plus, it's a model that can be used with reams of data or on a scrap of paper. It just requires the right questions to drive thoughtfulness and choice.

As you can see from this illustration, applying this thinking will help you avoid some of the rabbit holes I mentioned earlier. It hones the focus on discovering your quest by asking five questions.

➡ Does the problem fit in with the **Purpose** of your business?

➡ Do you have the **Prowess** or unique advantages to solve this problem?

➡ Is there enough **Potential market** to make this problem worthwhile?

➡ Can you make sufficient **Profit** from finding a solution?

➡ And finally, is it the right **Time** to address this problem?

OK, that's four 'Ps' and a 'T', but Timing is so essential I've given it more space. If the four 'Ps' bring the problem into focus, the timing is the trigger that captures the moment.

So let's leap into them in more detail. Apply them to your business as you go. The outcome is the central part of the diagram above: the Quest, your Quest. It should form a succinct sentence that sums up your direction, your Focus.

PURPOSE: WHAT YOU'RE IN BUSINESS FOR

This is what should drive all actions and, if clearly defined, will help innovation succeed. Clarify your purpose, and the rest becomes much easier. You may have the best solution or endless capabilities, but if the purpose isn't there, if the will isn't there among your team, if the direction isn't there, it's going to be very hard work indeed.

Defining the purpose in itself may be trickier than you imagine, and it's essential you get it right. In a term that is particularly free from passion, businesses often refer to this as 'strategic fit': does the problem fit the desired direction of the business? It's here we get into the murky waters of a company's mission and its vision. The purpose of the innovation, the purpose of solving that problem, must align with the overall mission and vision. No innovation will ever succeed if not driven by belief from the organisation behind it. Wishy-washy though some mission and vision statements can be, ask yourself:

➡ Does this problem we're solving fit in with what the company is doing now? (Mission)

➡ In the future, will this problem we're solving help change how you want the world to be? (Vision)

You should sense-check it against the values of the company. Does it meet the business's commitment to quality, to sustainability, to integrity?

It is your job as innovator-in-chief (the person sufficiently interested in innovation to be reading this book) to get behind the innovations you genuinely and wholeheartedly believe in and, therefore, get the rest of the team behind them too.

Example Purpose statements that I like are freely available on the website www.entrepreneur-within.com.

PROWESS: RECOGNISING YOUR UNFAIR ADVANTAGE

A real, valuable problem that you've identified doesn't necessarily mean a real, valuable source of growth. What *ikigai* perfectly articulates is the other side of the coin, which is all about you as a brand, a business, or an intrapreneur. Not all problems are right for all businesses to tackle.

This is the moment to think about your current competencies, strengths, backstory, heritage, and all of the elements that make up your business's DNA. What is your 'unfair advantage'? What are the unique capabilities you have which give you a chance to become the best in the world at solving this problem?

This goes to the core of your brand or business to identify what you can uniquely bring to develop a solution. What does your business have that no other business can replicate right now? Is it the fact you've successfully launched in this area before? Or perhaps enjoy access to a key market? Is it years of learning in a technology? Or is it the company culture?

It could be that there are individuals in the organisation who have the experience or knowledge, or there's a unique combination of skills and talent to harness. It could be a remarkable set of connections. It all builds a deeper and richer understanding of the problem. Can you find the in-depth knowledge to solve it?

And it's time to be honest. It's easy to be blinded by our own sense of self rather than taking an objective view that sets us apart from our competitors. Think about:

➡ What are the reasons to believe we can (uniquely) do this?
➡ Do we truly understand the competitors and how we stack up against them?
➡ What's in our history that provides the credibility or offers the tailwind to help us succeed?

It could be considered a 'feasibility' test. It ensures that this business has the capability to take on that problem.

Example Prowess statements that I like are freely available on the website www.entrepreneur-within.com.

POTENTIAL: ASSESSING HOW BIG THE PROBLEM REALLY IS

Potential is simple. Is there going to be a big enough market? Much has been written about defining the Total Addressable Market (TAM) and this is often the first question many prospective investors will ask. The problem with this method is that it is often calculated using existing market data. It may not only be inaccurate but cannot cope with the uncertainty of market disruption. Remember that data only looks backwards.

What we need to consider instead is the Total Addressable Problem (TAP) and think creatively about the broader need and the multiple answerable categories within. It doesn't necessarily make for an easy data trawl, but does provide a much wider and likely more realistic size of prize in the long term. You need to figure out WHO the audience is, and then how big the underlying problem is among that audience.

A well-known example to point out here is Uber. In 2008, when Uber pitched for investment, the taxi and limousine service market in the US was valued at $4.2 billion. Many investors passed on the investment opportunity because the industry was seen as too small to deliver a compelling return on investment. Today, the global ridesharing market is predicted to be $243 billion by 2028, and Uber has revised its market to be all vehicle and public transport trips, a market worth $5.7 trillion. There are plenty of tools that can be used to assess the size of the problem area. I've made some direct links available at www. entrepreneur-within.com, but first, consider what you need to find out about the market size and how you'll get to that answer. Often, it's about combining several groups of data. In the UK, I've found the Office for National Statistics,

Statista, Companies House, Similar Web and Facebook Ad Archive all to be particularly useful. But don't forget the power of direct research and speaking to your customers, as we'll see in the Results chapter, but here we're focussing on ensuring we're hitting a decent market.

The question remains simple: Is the problem big enough to warrant attention from our business? Is it big enough to satisfy our growth ambition? What is sufficient for a fledgling entrepreneur is likely to be very different for an established multinational. The answer will ultimately come down to the size of your ambition and any specific goals or objectives you set for new ventures.

PROFIT: CALCULATING HOW MUCH VALUE CAN BE UNLOCKED

The size of the addressable problem is, however, only one question. The other critical question is: is the problem real enough that people will pay to solve it? Organisations need to rapidly assess the available profit pools, and which are the most compelling places along a value chain in which to invest. Larger businesses should already have tools available to assess the potential size of turnover. They'll probably have an idea of the variable costs and the operational costs required to then work out what remaining profit there is to compete for. For a new problem area, what is the white space to get at?

And let's be clear: instead of profit, if you're working within a public sector or not-for-profit organisation, the calculation here could be about the public good. Will a new initiative really reduce childhood obesity? Will a change in curriculum genuinely improve literacy?

But how can we quickly test these assumptions? If you have a direct-to-consumer website, put the product up and see if people click 'Add to cart' at a certain price. That can be done at a very early stage. You can get access to a huge amount of people. Interrogate Companies House for data on similar companies: How are your competitors faring with a similar product? For manufactured products, you can reverse engineer them to get a pretty good guess at the costs involved. And don't underestimate taking people out for a coffee. Speak to your network, your ecosystem, to see if there is real profit in it.

There are countless problems facing individuals and populations every day, but even when a real problem exists, the impact of the problem can vary wildly. Some issues are mild irritants, while others cause real pain. And then, what causes 'pain' for one person might only be a mild irritant for someone else. The key is to understand – for your target audience – what a genuine pain point is (where you need a painkiller) versus a niggle (where a vitamin may suffice) that they comfortably work around.

For example, Kimberly-Clark launched Huggies Convertibles in 2003, a hybrid nappy and nappy-pant designed for both usages. Parents no longer had to buy two different format types. In reality, it didn't function particularly well (as I learned), nor did it solve a major problem, it just fixed a niggle for a short period of time. Ripping a pant product (when the contents dictate a lie-down change is required) wasn't a big enough deal to warrant a less convenient pant format for other occasions.

As the nappy-pant example shows, sometimes asking your audience really isn't the answer because what we perceive as annoying frequently proves not to be the case when push comes to shove. It needs to be a pain point for which we really will change our behaviour. The only way to understand this is to get close to customers in their real lives and understand the full purchase-consumption journey. OK, no more nappy chat.

TALES, TRAPS AND TIPS
JAKE ZIM

Jake Zim is the Chief Marketing Officer of Another Axiom, makers of the world's biggest VR game, Gorilla Tag. *Jake formerly served as vice president of virtual reality at Sony Pictures Entertainment. Before Sony, Jake was vice president of digital marketing at Fox.*

ON HAVING A CLEAR FOCUS FROM THE TOP

Focus is crucial for young companies navigating the dynamic landscapes and convergence of new technology, and entertainment. In these rapidly evolving industries, maintaining a clear vision and concentrated efforts is crucial for survival and success. By dedicating resources to a specific niche or core product, young companies can build a strong foundation, establish a unique identity, and effectively compete. Diverging attention too early can dilute efforts, hinder innovation, and ultimately compromise the company's ability to capitalise on emerging opportunities.

ON DEVELOPING A NETWORK OF PROBLEM SOLVERS

Developing relationships and a network of problem solvers that you can count on when challenges arise is crucial for navigating the complexities of building new businesses. A strong network of collaborators can provide valuable insights, support and resources, helping you overcome obstacles and achieve your goals. By fostering a collaborative environment and seeking out diverse perspectives, you can increase your chances of success in the competitive and ever-changing business landscape.

ON BEING OKAY WITH FAILURE

You've got to be okay with failure, over and over. At some point, the pivots that you make have to point you in the direction of a pot of gold. So if that's not the direction you're going in, then you need to adjust quickly and realign so you're on the right path.

TIMING: PINPOINTING THE WHEN

'The best way to predict the future is to invent it.'

ALAN KAY, COMPUTER SCIENTIST

THE MAGIC REALLY HAPPENS, however, when you can align on a problem area that fits all the four Ps, when the Purpose, Prowess, Potential and Profit overlap. It's a problem that fits the mission, you've got a unique advantage, and it seems there are sufficient people who are willing to pay for it. Your research suggests that you may make a profit from it. But there's one thing that is critical for success: timing.

Entrepreneur Bill Gross, in one of the most watched TED Talks of all time, argues that timing is the single biggest reason why start-ups succeed. In fact, according to Bill's calculations, timing accounted for 42 per cent of the difference between success and failure. Ahead of team and execution, ahead of the idea, ahead of the business model and ahead of funding. The archives of innovation history are full of examples of good ideas launched at the wrong time, either too soon or too late.

The online grocery business Webvan filed for bankruptcy in 2001; a year later pets.com went the same way. The Xerox Alto personal computer was launched in 1973. AT&T developed a videophone in 1927, and the first electric cars were developed in the 1830s. Really. With the tagline: 'Look! No horse nor ox, yet it moves!'

Understanding the strength and direction of consumer and technological trends is invaluable in helping assess the right moment. Asking customers what they want is often too late. And, like all innovation, the right time for one organisation might be different for another. The prowess required might change over time.

For new ventures, targeting a small, niche audience and establishing a beachhead makes sense. To do so, you need to get in early, and then build, iterate and take advantage of the tailwind. One of the issues with larger organisations is that they are often late to the party.

Balancing the ride of being too early, not having enough room to scale, being too late, and increased competition, is an art more than a science. Timing is essentially about realistic expectations at your location on the curve. Early on, you're looking at niche audiences, potentially with a long lag before scale develops. It took Oatly fifteen years before it finally made it into mainstream consciousness.

Patience is another aspect often forgotten in timing. Corporations rarely have business models that allow for comparatively slow-growth innovation, so ideas die before they have enough chance to gain traction. Recognising the nature of the niche and the likely time lag is a fundamental part of the planning.

On the flip side, coming in later on brings challenges of sustaining the growth and rejuvenating a potentially levelling category. This demands much greater investment in continued innovation and margin enhancement. Simply put, plan your timing with open eyes to where you are hitting the curve.

The timing and trends question can be applied to each of the Four Ps.

➡ Are these trends moving towards or away from our vision for the future?

➡ Are our 'unfair advantages' becoming more or less relevant?

➡ Is the potential market size growing or shrinking?

➡ Are customers becoming willing to spend more or less to solve the problem?

TALES, TRAPS AND TIPS
NICOLA CHANCE-THOMPSON

Nicola Chance-Thompson MBE, DL, FRSA is the CEO and Trustee of the multi-award-winning Piece Hall in Halifax, Yorkshire. Nicky has worked on major regeneration projects after a background in creative arts, advertising and consulting.

ON BRAVE LEADERSHIP

Leadership has to come from the top. It has to have a specific mindset of 'can do', not 'let's see what we can't do'. You have to have people who have a mindset of outcomes, not outputs.

ON BUILDING A SHARED VISION

At The Piece Hall, we've managed to form a coalition of willing people who share our dream, who share our vision and who are really open to new ideas, new creativity, and new thinking. This shared vision has enabled great things to happen.

ON INNOVATION AND CHANGE

One trap is believing that everybody wants the change to happen. If you're looking at any transformation project, you need to be sure the key decision-makers are actively behind the change and agree.

ON BUILDING FOCUS IN A TEAM

There's a certain group of people I'll do the dreaming with, and then there's a certain group of people I go into action with. It prevents distraction. I always say, "Let's not let perfection get in the way of really good, let's get going".

ON NAVIGATING INNOVATION CHANGE

Some people will get on the bus with you, other people will try and take the tyres off the bus. You have to deal with those saboteurs super quickly. If you can get influencers or champions internally to help take those 'maybes' along, it prevents quite a lot of resistance because the misinformation or disinformation that can arise is dealt with.

If you can settle on a problem that is focused on those four things and nods to where the trends are going for each one, this will provide your quest ('quest' being a position statement, 'problem' is negative), the direction of your journey and a clear goal. It is the quest you need to fall in love with. By reframing it as a quest, you can bring onboard other people, the company, the customers and the world. JFK didn't say: 'Actually, we're struggling to get to the moon; let's hope we do so by 1969 and beat the Russians.' He did say: 'We choose to go to the moon. We choose to go to the moon in this decade and do the other things, not because they are easy, but because they are hard.'

Your quest as an innovator-in-chief starts with this story. Your summary of Purpose, Potential, Prowess and Profit will lead you to write your quest, the focal point. Clarity of vision is incredibly powerful. You have your problem; now, we turn to solving it.

START YOUR QUEST

Focus is really all about choices: choice of the right problem that can deliver the right value for which the business is right for solving. There are myriad different ways to reach a point of focus, but using the Four Ps (Purpose, Prowess, Potential, Profit) and considering timing is a clear way to start. If you think about it, this helps answer the three fundamental questions of WHY, WHERE and WHEN:

WHY?
This unearths the business requirements for innovation, plus answering why we're well-placed to solve the problem. In our Four Ps model, this is Purpose PLUS Prowess. In other words, what's the point of this whole endeavour?

WHERE?
Have we spotted a big enough customer problem that would be sufficiently profitable if we solved it successfully? This is potential PLUS Profit.

WHEN?

Understand why we should solve this problem now and consider whether the trends are moving in our favour. This is about timing.

Once you've answered these three admittedly important questions, we're perfectly placed to move into the HOW, which is what the next chapter, Originality, is all about.

But let's not kid ourselves; in an ideal world, we'd start at the very beginning and work through Focus first. In reality, innovation is an iterative process, a bit messy and with multiple circle-backs. Chances are you've got an idea or a pipeline or are even in the launch phase. That doesn't mean that Focus isn't relevant. On the contrary, taking the time to step back and clarify will ultimately yield bigger, better results that innovation should be all about. No more rabbits to chase or rabbit holes to avoid.

THE ENTREPRENEUR WITHIN PART 2

FORGE YOUR WAY

KEY TAKEAWAYS

➡ Choose your innovation quest wisely, and be sure to apply your focus to the problem, and not to the solution.

➡ The right problem is found at the intersection of the 4Ps: Purpose, Prowess, Potential and Profit.

➡ Timing is so important, and not always in your control. Always ask: why now?

➡ Potential can change dramatically with time. The 'Total Addressable Problem' might be much bigger than existing data shows.

➡ Remember that speed does not equal velocity, and also that rabbits move fast! Be selective, be focused.

QUESTIONS TO REFLECT ON

➡ Is the purpose of your business completely clear? Would it help to revisit the business's mission and vision statements?

➡ What do you believe are the three biggest problems facing your target customers today? How is the market changing?

➡ Does your problem, or potential problems, really play into your Purpose or Prowess? Can you tackle this better than anyone else?

➡ Write a problem statement in this structure: How might we... [name the problem] through or by... [ways to solve the problem]. It will help you hone your quest. It should be one sentence or two.

FREE RESOURCES

At www.entrepreneur-within.com/focus you'll find:

➡ Some of my favourite purpose statements and problem statements.

➡ Links to helpful tools to help calculate the potential size of a problem.

➡ A downloadable infographic on the 4Ps (and a T) of Focus.

ORIGINALITY

NO MAGIC STARDUST REQUIRED

'Where patterns are broken,
new worlds emerge.'
TULI KUPFERBERG

ENGAGE INTEREST, CAPTURE ATTENTION

Having tackled the WHY, the WHERE and the WHEN of innovation in the Focus chapter, Originality moves on to the HOW. How might we fulfil the opportunity we've identified? And how do we successfully fulfil the opportunity with sufficient distinction and differentiation to rise to the top?

The aim here is to think differently, to stand out, and to capture the attention of your potential customers. Life is busy and full of intrusions. I'm often reminded of the dog in the Pixar movie *Up*: smart and erudite but constantly distracted by a squirrel. The human brain, especially now, has endless distractions. In 2015, Microsoft infamously stated that the average human attention span is now 8.25 seconds. It's not true, although the best estimate of 20 years of studies isn't particularly more encouraging. In that time, computer scientists and psychologists believe that the average time that a person can focus on one thing has dropped from around 2.5 minutes to around 45 seconds. The fact that you've made it to the end of this paragraph without checking your phone (which people do on average 58 times a day), therefore, is a testament to marathon focus. Go you!

The popular narrative is that humans are becoming less and less capable of concentrating and giving anything more than their glancing attention; hence, the explosion of micro-messaging and short-form videos and the inbred terror among brand owners of creating content designed for anything above a few seconds.

The reality, thank goodness, is different. As Shane Snow eloquently articulated in a 2023 *Forbes* article, attention span is irrelevant; interest is not. Humans will bestow their attention – and plenty of it – on stories that capture their imaginations, emotions and quest for novelty.

This thirst for interest matters whether you're an influencer or entertainer, journalist, teacher or a business leader. And especially to you, our innovator-in-chief, who is planning to launch a new product or venture. Coming up with new ideas can often be the easy bit; your challenge is to obsess about how you elevate them to shine through AND sustain the interest of your audience. Engage them, innovatively, and you earn their attention.

Of course, the competition for interest is immense. The ever-increasing pace of technological change is shortening product life cycles and proliferating new generations of products. New routes to market and an expanding marketplace open businesses up to genuinely global competition. At the same time, trends in socio-environmental consciousness and the quest for self-identity are fuelling the rise of SMEs and their 'authentic storytelling brands'.

While this brings unparalleled opportunities, it also has colossal implications around the sheer number of innovations showing up and the pace at which they need to monetise to survive. The UK Intellectual Property Office alone processed 19,486 applications in 2022. Just imagine how many will be processed when AI gets to work.

HOW ORIGINAL IS ORIGINAL?

What Picasso meant by this quote (right) isn't disingenuous; instead, it's about the benefits of taking a shortcut to knowledge. Steve Jobs was fond of the quote, too. Copying, producing a facsimile, adds nothing to your knowledge,

> *'Capture my interest, and you won't need to worry about my attention span.'*
> KUSHANDWIZDOM

> *'Lesser artists copy; great artists steal.'*
> PABLO PICASSO

or the potential of improving on the original. Stealing means you imbibe it, learn from it, develop it further.

But… and it's a sizeable 'but', sometimes, it can be OK to copy. It's certainly easier to copy and surf the wave already generated by others. Instagram Stories followed Snapchat, Indiegogo cloned Kickstarter, and Google quickly followed Amazon with its Home smart device. And then Apple with its HomePod. It happens all the time, and there have been many great successes.

And sometimes, as we referenced in Focus, it can be OK to bring less creative innovations to market. If they fit well within existing capability and can deliver substantial returns on investment by extending usage into new occasions or category segments, then why not? It may not fundamentally change category behaviour, but it can make money.

The FORGE methodology is suited to all types of innovation, including those not straying too far from the core business. But, as in the spirit of Focus, this book is designed for those occasions when we're looking at the genuinely new, not when keeping up is enough.

If you really want to stand out from the crowd of new innovations brought to market each year, if you really want to cut through and capture interest, then you need originality. Lots of it. We must step outside conventional thinking and traditional wisdom.

To borrow a quote from Albert Einstein: 'Problems cannot be solved by thinking within the methodology in which the problems were created.'

NO MAGIC STARDUST REQUIRED

The challenge is that we all grow up. And, in growing up, we typically shed an innate belief in our own powers of creative thought and originality. When you mention the word 'innovation', many of us immediately parcel that up to 'the work of creative types, probably somewhere in Silicon Valley'. We shut off potential before it's been given a chance because we misunderstand the origins of great –

and original – innovation. The good news is... it's there, all around us and within you. It's just a matter of unlocking it.

Time to bust some myths...

MYTH 1: INNOVATION REQUIRES MAGIC STARDUST

Creativity is not a rare superpower bestowed upon true mavericks. In reality, truly new ideas rarely emerge spontaneously from the air or pop into someone's head. I think of innovation as making previously unseen connections. In doing so, suddenly, we're playing to one of the great strengths that we have as humans. Our brains are naturally good at connecting things and forming links.

Sometimes, however, too good. Our brains take shortcuts to reinforce perceived links and are trained to work within our man-made boundaries, such as education and process. The result? We are programmed to artificially contain ourselves in the world of what we already know.

This realisation is well documented by Edward De Bono[7] – author of eighty-five books – who coined the term 'lateral thinking'. The main thrust of the premise was that creativity rests on establishing conditions where barriers are removed and where new links or connections can be made. In other words, conditions that allow ANYONE to become an ideas expert and for the magic to flow.

To do this, we can utilise creative thinking techniques, and I've included some of my favourite in the FURNACE toolkit later in this chapter. These techniques break down our existing beliefs, assumptions and 'rivers of thought'. As Orson Scott Card so eloquently puts it, 'We question all of our beliefs, except for the ones we really believe in, and those we never think to question.'

MYTH 2: ALL NEW IDEAS WORTH DOING HAVE BEEN DONE

Well, if this were true, then a whole industry of innovation specialists, practitioners and investors would be made redundant at a swipe. However, we only need to look around to witness the value of innovations in changing

'Thank goodness I was never sent to school; it would have rubbed off some of the originality.'
BEATRIX POTTER

TALES, TRAPS AND TIPS
ZANDRA MOORE

Zandra Moore is the co-founder and CEO of Panintelligence and a tech entrepreneur specialising in data analytics and AI. Zandra's unwavering energy has led to the creation of LeanIn Leeds, The No Code Lab, The Lifted Project and the Yorkshire Growth Tech Group, all with a focus of supporting and championing female representation in the tech industry.

ON ROLE MODELS

You can't be what you can't see.

ON TESTING FRAMEWORKS

It's so important to have a framework to understand the customer, and to help structure your thoughts. What do I need to know that I don't already know? How do I test these hypotheses outside of my organisation? Who do I need to speak to to get validation of that pain? If your ideal customer isn't really pinned down, the data you get back will not be valuable enough.

ON PRIORITISING CUSTOMER FEEDBACK

The benefit of having business customers for software is that they are very vocal about wanting to know what your roadmap is. They are very vocal about what they believe will add the most value to them. So we get a huge amount of customer feedback all of the time. The challenge for us is prioritising all of those ideas from the market and deciding which will drive the greatest value and will also future-proof our product.

ON PREPARING THE FUTURE ROADMAP

We'll always present what we call roadmap items – things that the customer does not necessarily drive, but that we believe they will ask for in the future. We get ahead and ask for feedback on what they would value the most about that innovation.

ON GIVING THE DEVELOPERS FREEDOM

We have innovation days every month. We take an idea and give the development team free rein to build it and unlock their brains. This interrupts the pattern of delivering code and allows us to think about the impact on entire solutions. You can do some really crazy things with innovation days, and everything is celebrated. It's all good learning and really helps us.

ON FOSTERING AN INNOVATIVE CULTURE

You have to have an open and supportive culture where people feel safe. Without a safe culture, it's very, very hard to drive innovation and have an appetite for risk. It is critical that you know how to create that culture of safety, how to treat people, and how to make them feel about their contribution.

ON WHY INNOVATION ECOSYSTEMS ARE ESSENTIAL

Being part of a working ecosystem is the single most important factor. I used to be an invisible founder. I had no idea. I didn't know what I didn't know, and I had no idea about raising money. I had no idea about who could help and support me. It was only when I was literally dragged out of my business to participate in a tech accelerator, that this world just opened up. The biggest factor that burns early-stage start-up founders out is they spend too much time talking to the wrong people because it's the wrong stage for them.

ON GETTING SUPPORT

When you start to ask more questions, it accelerates my personal development, my network, my confidence, and my certainty that I can afford to take those risks and be supported. Most people don't do this because they've not got the right advice and they've not got the right support.

ON THE IMPORTANCE OF DIVERSITY

Innovation comes from diversity: diverse thoughts, diverse ideas, diverse experiences, diverse skills.

attitudes, behaviours and marketplaces. We recognise there will always be a problem that needs solving and for which people are prepared to pay for a solution. It comes back to truly understanding the customer, as well as the scale and scope of their problem.

The myth about having to always come up with a new idea often manifests in the response: 'We've tried this before.' Maybe you have, maybe this is something that looks similar but is different, and as is often the case, the time for this idea has now come. Thinking like this signals a failure of imagination and is often the root cause of feeling 'stuck'.

It's easy to think that a decade ago, kids' luggage was all about funkier designs and storage, and then Trunki came along. It reimagined luggage as solving storage AND travel entertainment AND child mobility problems. Removing the category blinkers and connecting different parent pains throughout their travel experiences enabled a ground-breaking innovation that has grown into a multi-million pound global brand. Read my interview with Rob Law, founder of Trunki.

MYTH 3: ORIGINALITY IS ALL ABOUT PRODUCT
There is a lingering perception that innovation only lies in what the customer can see. While most people would readily acknowledge that this is not true, how often are the multiple dimensions of innovation really considered? A pretty widespread and accepted concept that illustrates the point is the 'ten types of innovation', as defined by Doblin. It demonstrates how innovation can relate to 'Configuration' (profit, network, structure, process), 'Offering' (product performance, product system) and 'Experience' (customer engagement, brand, channel, service). So when a business identifies a need for innovation, ask if they are mainly concerned with sourcing or systems, improving experience, or do they actually mean 'we need a new product offering'?

We've touched on Uber before, but it serves to illustrate my point here, too. Uber is not offering a new service. They get you from A to B in a car with a driver. What's innovative is the way to access the service (the route to market) AND their supply chain of drivers AND their customer experience.

The growing number of purpose-led brands are more recent high-profile examples. What's interesting here is how some of these brands – such as Tony's Chocolonely – have delivered originality by innovating their supply chains rather than creating any genuinely new type of product. It's a very nice chocolate (and in funky packaging with interesting flavours and formats), but the originality lies in the supply story they tell, which has a great impact.

It would be remiss here not to mention the popsicle hotline. If you haven't installed one already at your house, let me explain. A hotel in Los Angeles called Magic Castle Hotel installed a phone line by the pool that allowed kids to call the hotline and demand a popsicle. A smartly dressed waiter would then appear with the ice lolly. Cute idea. But what it did do was earn thousands of column inches and turn a somewhat mediocre hotel into one that kids would demand their parents take them to. It was innovation in service and marketing and cost almost nothing.

Profitable original ideas can be applied across your value chain as well as your supply chain. You could discover innovation through your business's systems and processes, on the customer experience of the business and its offerings, or through the offering that surrounds your core product.

Ask yourself:

➡ What other ways can we deliver our product? What is the easiest way to get it into the customer's hands?

➡ Do we need to tell our story better? Does the brand reflect the quest we're on? Does it resonate with our customers?

➡ Can we engage our customers in a more compelling way? Is our product coveted, and can our brand promise that?

➡ How can we amplify the value of our product or service? Your customers are key to understanding this element.

➡ Do we need to change the structure of the supply and company assets to maximise profit and offer an improved or better-priced product?

➡ How can we build an ecosystem for the core offering that the consumer will be part of? What complementary services or products can we offer?

With the myths busted, let's talk practically about how you go about thinking originally and capturing that all-too-valuable customer interest.

TALES, TRAPS AND TIPS
JUSTIN PETSZAFT

*Justin Petszaft is the Founder and MD at
Atom Group. A theoretical physicist by
training, Justin's data-driven and evidence-
backed approach to business has helped him
launch many successful spirits brands and
e-commerce ventures.*

ON LINKING MVPS TO COMEDY

We could learn a lot about Minimum Viable Products (MVPs) from
comedy. There's no amount of prep you can do to ensure a joke is
funny. You can't make a comedy routine sitting in your bedroom
writing and rewriting it, you just need to get in front of an audience.
And it's only then that you find out: Is that shit? Or is it funny? But
people are so afraid to get out there.

ON WHY SCHOOL STIFLES INNOVATION

Everything about the current school system teaches you that
every problem has a 'right' solution and a 'right' way to approach
it. If you're wrong, you don't get the mark or you fail the exam.
And that teaches us a fear of failure and a fear of looking stupid.
It's incredibly unhelpful if you have an economy that requires
innovation and adaptation.

ON DISCOVERING ORIGINALITY AT THE FRINGE

People find it hard to innovate because they've never really
had to think original thoughts. We've accidentally developed
an organisational and societal monoculture. My advice? Go to
the most different culture that you can and get all of your ideas
challenged. Good ideas are always going to come from the fringe.
Almost all ideas on the fringe are terrible ideas, but 100 per cent of
the good ideas will come from the fringe.

ORIGINALITY IN ACTION

'Nothing is more dangerous than an idea when it is the only one you have.'

EMILE-AUGUSTE CHARTIER (KNOWN AS ALAIN)

THE STARTING POINT FOR GREAT IDEAS is always a clear direction. After reading the Focus chapter, you should have uncovered your quest from the vault of confusion. But how many of us can just come up with great ideas on the hoof just because we're told to?

In the pages that follow, you'll find a practical guide for coming up with original and distinctive ideas in the real world. This includes suggestions for creating a fertile environment for ideas to take hold, techniques for boosting creative thought and tips for overcoming the creative blockers that can often arise in larger organisations.

1. CREATE THE CONDITIONS FOR CREATIVITY TO TAKE HOLD

CREATING SPACE AND STIMULATING MINDS

Creativity is the ability to think beyond habit and conditioning. No one is going to be at their most creative when sitting at their desk tackling their inbox, fidgeting around a boardroom table or feeling the pressure to impress the boss. Getting the most out of people requires putting effort into opening up minds. And this doesn't necessarily have to mean a room of beanbags and Post-it notes (though those certainly have their place).

It's about putting people at ease, drawing a line between ideation and day-to-day work, and creating an environment that stimulates rather than stifles.

When you want to stimulate divergent thoughts, some simple actions can make all the difference:

➡ Actively step away from inboxes and desks. That means phones off and ideally out of sight from the normal workspace.

➡ Encourage building on ideas by using 'yes, and' rather than 'erm, but'. This classic improvisation technique encourages playful building on ideas right from the outset.

➡ Include a broad mix of individuals – genuine diversity of background, thinking, gender, age, race and seniority – ideally include some who have 'less skin in the game' and can, therefore, think more freely.

➡ Think hard about which stakeholders need to be included in a creative session and how everyone can feel free to take part as equals – job titles should be left at the door.

➡ Find ways to immerse yourself in the problem and put yourself in the customer's shoes. There are many ways to do this, with some as simple as following relevant influencers, meeting customers or reading previous research.

➡ Take time to look outside your industry and see how others might tackle similar problems. Don't force this, but realise that more diverse perspectives often produce more original thought. Have you invited any 'outsiders'?

If you think your organisation is doing enough to create the conditions that enable innovation to thrive, just pause the congratulations for a moment. According to Barclays' Tim Heard, '75 per cent of corporations feel they promote an innovative culture, yet 75 per cent of entrepreneurs leave corporates because they feel stifled.'

THOUGHTS ARE NOT IDEAS

We all have thoughts. Loads of them. The problem is that sometimes we judge thoughts as though they are ideas. This might seem pedantic, but it's a critical point to grasp.

You have far more thoughts than

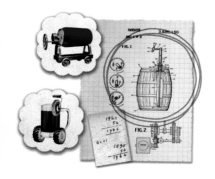

you do ideas. Thoughts typically precede ideas, they are not well defined and they tend to be relevant in a particular moment. This leads to thoughts being interpreted (very) differently by people with different perspectives. And we all have different perspectives. We all have a unique way of making sense of the world. For example, when I say, 'Let's build a beer machine,' it's very likely that I'm imagining something different to you.

An idea, on the other hand, is more defined. To forge breakthrough innovation, we need to become very specific and intentional about what an idea actually is. It's vital that ideas are adequately captured in such a way that they are fully formed rather than throwaway comments. Anyone needs to be able to pick up an idea – physically or virtually – and be clear about what it is.

The best innovation teams store those fully formed ideas in a central repository – let's call it an ideas bank – ready and waiting to be picked up when the time is right. The trends we discussed in Focus continue to change, and it's likely that people will change too, so ideas need to be well documented enough to be instantly understandable and actionable if/when the time comes.

A well-defined idea is likely to include the following:

» Idea headline
» Proposed solution to the problem
» Top features of the idea
» Key benefits explained
» The experience the idea offers
» The value (including price)
» Potential partnerships
» A visualisation or even prototype
» A clear idea of the customer

2. IGNITE THE IDEAS

The first rule of thumb for a great idea is that it doesn't have to start from a blank canvas. Ideas crop up in organisations all the time and are parked, nurtured, abandoned, delayed or simply lost along the way.

So, where better to start than dusting off everything that's already out there? This not only gets you off to a running start but ensures that you're not reinventing the wheel and wasting energy. Bring along anything that already exists – you have an ideas bank, remember? – and share it with the group as a starter-for-ten. Encourage everyone to improve, build and combine with other ideas.

Next, it's time for a bit of a group splurge, a 'get it off your chest', a 'first burst' session. It's an opportunity for everyone to articulate ideas they've been carrying around in their heads or have been sparked by the conversations so far.

It can feel uncomfortable, but it's critical to let the ideas flow unstructured initially. This is the phase of divergent thinking, whereby you allow minds to wander. Park all the usual commercial constraints and ensure that no idea is shut down. This allows the problem to be explored from every angle and fully frees the brain to be its most creative.

BRING OUT THE SPRINGBOARDS

At the point that those first-burst ideas struggle to flow, it's time to offer some focus to the ideation process. I like to use 'springboards', different jumping-off points to develop ideas for solving problems.

In an ideation session with a larger group, each team could choose a different springboard from which to begin. For example, imagine you are thinking about launching a new phone. The springboards could be 'lifesaving' or 'tribal gathering', 'personal safety', 'entertain me', 'make friends', or 'grow with me'. What does a phone look like whose sole purpose is 'personal safety'? You can immediately see how these springboards can inspire different directions of thinking. One team would look at marketing, while

FURNACE TOOLKIT

EVEN FOR THE MOST NATURALLY creative groups, the ideas flow will eventually run dry. When this happens, there are numerous creative techniques to stimulate more thinking. The FURNACE toolkit is a collation of the best techniques I've learned to uncork a fresh stream of ideas. More resources and tools can be found for free, at www.entrepreneur-within.com. And have fun!

FLIP IT

This is about delving into the assumptions that underpin your problem and then examining the current range of solutions that attempt to address it. Then, ask yourselves what would happen if the opposite of that assumption was true. At first, flipping these assumptions might seem silly, funny, or even just random, but keep going to see where the art of the possible can take you.

UTOPIA

This method transports you into a world of limitless resources. In that world, what is the most perfect solution to your problem that you could dream of? How could you apply those limitless resources to your problem? This enables the mind to expand and consider possibilities that seem ridiculous until they might spark further thought later down the line.

RANDOM

It is exactly that. Find something, anything, that at first glance has no relation to your problem at all. This might be a random word found by opening a book at a random page. Now, find links with how it might potentially be used to address your problem. Be creative. Brainstorm as many as you can, no matter how random or silly they might appear to be.

NEGATIVE

This technique encourages you to think of the worst possible ways to solve your problem. Come up with ideas that could make the problem even worse. Have some fun. Then take a fresh look to see if this unlocked something new to be built upon for a more creative solution.

ADJACENT

Consider similar, related markets or industries that face a similar type of problem, customer or occasion. How do people solve this problem in an adjacent market? What solutions do other companies in other industries adopt to solve a similar problem? Is there anything that can be learned from studying these approaches? Can anything be brought back to your problem from these adjacent worlds?

CONNECT

Create an original solution by connecting multiple existing solutions that already exist. The solutions might not be from your market or directly related to your problem, but connecting multiple existing products or services together might unlock a fresh way to approach your particular problem. Do not limit yourself to two or three connections; keep going with as many as possible, which, when combined in a unique way, might directly help to address your problem.

EXPRESS

This invites you to have some fun through a different dimension. For example, this might be acting out your problem with teammates, developing a model of your problem with Lego, writing a poem to express your problem, or even getting the paint pots out and creating a watercolour. Re-expression of your problem through different media helps unlock new neural pathways and brings fresh insight and thinking about how to develop an original solution.

another could spring off from technological advances. The aim is to then gather the best ideas from each springboard and bring them together for the 'prioritisation and perfection' phase.

3. COME BACK TO REALITY

If the steps above are all about divergent thinking, this is the time to start to converge those ideas and overlay more rational considerations to start transforming ideas into more commercially meaningful opportunities. Only now is it time to throw in a dose of reality to the ideas.

The order in which you approach this stage is entirely fluid. You can build it into the ideation event or tackle it afterwards; you can invite customer feedback or apply commercial constraints first. What's important is that you're fully into convergent thinking, with the end goal of delivering compelling, highly original, but realistic concepts that can then be progressed to market in Results. Ask yourself:

A) HAVE WE ANSWERED THE BRIEF?

First, reference back to Focus and rigorously check each idea that answers the brief. Consider some kind of traffic lighting exercise against a set of key questions.

➡ **Purpose.** How well does the idea fit the overall mission and vision of the business?

➡ **Prowess.** How well can we deliver this idea versus competitors? What is our unfair advantage?

➡ **Potential.** How big could this idea be? Does it solve the entire problem for everyone? Or is it best suited to a niche?

➡ **Profit.** Are future customers likely to pay sufficiently for this solution that it could become profitable?

➡ **Timing.** Is your audience ready? Are the trends moving in our favour?

Customer input at this stage can be valuable but not always feasible within budgets. If possible, a rapid screening methodology (overnight screenings can be a great tool to fit within a two-day workshop) helps shorten the list and highlight the strengths and weaknesses of ideas. Equally, inviting customers in for quick qualitative groups can also shed light and provide optimisation opportunities. For those with a smaller budget, there are plenty of creative ways to get around this, such as using in-house employees, agency partners, customer panels and even friends and family (within the target audience), as long as you are clear and consistent in the questions that you're asking.

B) CAN WE MAKE OUR IDEAS STRONGER?

Have we considered the multiple dimensions of innovation in our quest to improve these ideas? Consider your ideas with regard to the customer target, the value proposition, plus the marketing, routes to market, operations and finance.

These multiple lenses talk exactly to 'Myth 3' mentioned earlier, that the assumption that innovation is all about the product. Look at the questions posed in that section, and apply them again to the final idea. Chances are you'll be able to hone the idea even more.

Innovation requires the full customer journey. Introducing the concept of innovation types is a useful way to stimulate additional ideas and stretch thinking. To ensure you're approaching innovation in its broadest sense, now consider your solution from each of these perspectives.

➡ **Customer**. It seems obvious, but it is critical. This is the importance of innovating to create a proposition and experience that's right for a particular customer group and their problem. Could this idea appeal to, or be even better for, another customer group?

➡ **Value proposition**. How do the benefits of this solution combine to add real value for our customers? What are all the elements that need to be there to solve the problem?

➡ **Marketing**. How do we best communicate the proposition? What is the messaging? Are there different ways of telling the story that can connect better with the customer? How do we cut through and grab attention?

TALES, TRAPS AND TIPS
ROB LAW

*Rob Law MBE is the founder and CEO of Trunki,
the brand behind the much-loved ride-on
suitcase for tots. His latest ventures include an
agency to help brands thrive on Amazon, and
Zeepy, an innovative clock to enhance natural
sleep in infants and young children.*

ON RESILIENCE AND REJECTION

New things are often rejected. For 'Trunki', I approached toy
companies, and they told me to go to luggage companies, who
in turn told me I'd invented a toy. The retailers simply passed it
around to different departments because no one wanted to take
the risk. I just had to keep going at it and try to find a different way.
For me, Trunki should be positioned as a lifestyle brand outside of
traditional categories, so I made my own website and sold through
catalogue companies. I still believed in the concept and liked the
idea of trying to run my own thing. So, when my first shipment
arrived, I quit my job as a design consultant and took the leap.

ON WHY YOU SHOULD ITERATE

Trunki has been copied so many times, but no one else has really
got traction in the market. What I've learnt is that you don't
need to go to market with an all-singing, all-dancing product.
Get something out there, and then take iterative steps. This also
keeps the competition on their toes the whole way through. Keep
launching updates and better versions.

ON GETTING TRACTION

Trying to get traction in the market was the hard part. I sent a press
release to an international design blog, and after being pubished it
opened the door to enquiries from Japan, Australia, and even the
Museum of Modern Art in New York, which was a big kudos thing
for me. They became my first international customer.

- ➡ **Routes to market.** How can we get this new product and service in front of the right customers? Is our existing go-to market strategy fit for purpose, or should we explore new ways to get this out there?
- ➡ **Operations.** This is anything related to supply, manufacturing and process. It's often the least readily considered dimension when innovating, but there are usually hidden ways to add value to customers and considerations here that could have a massive impact on the commercial viability of the venture.
- ➡ **Finance.** How does the customer pay (upfront, recurring, subscription)? Are there opportunities for bulk sales, promotions or value engineering to improve the concept?

C) SORTING THE WHEAT FROM THE CHAFF

Finally, it's time to call a day on the idea generation and switch the mindset towards refinement and prioritisation. A simple approach is:

- ➡ Give everyone involved the opportunity to see all the ideas and take time to reflect. This could be during a break or overnight if a two-day workshop.
- ➡ Group together ideas that feel similar or overlap. Don't overthink it; just a rough grouping will help people make sense of it all.
- ➡ Hone in on the favourites through the simple mechanism of voting (sticky dots, thumbs up, clap-o-meters, whatever takes your fancy). This is not scientific, but the energy will gravitate naturally towards the strongest ideas. People naturally vote with the customer and business realities in the backs of their minds.
- ➡ It's then a question of building up the best 'idea buckets' into something bigger. Do this by crunching together the best bits from multiple ideas, challenging assumptions and crafting them into more detailed and tangible concepts.

By the end of this stage, you're looking for a shortlist of, say, ten to twenty ideas that are real enough for anyone to understand. Anyone at all. Yes, your kids or partner, your meddling auntie or grumpy grandad.

D) LET THE IDEAS GROW

This is often called 'greenhousing'. And despite my resistance to turning a noun into a verb, it does make sense. It is the careful nurturing of new ideas, protecting them from the scythe or the storms that can come their way. This is required in large businesses, where the deletion of a line on a spreadsheet can mean the end of a new innovation.

However, the idea requires protection even before we speak about budgeting. We need to get some tests out there. Judging and assessing come in the next chapter, in Results, based on not a hunch or a disappointing boardroom meeting but real-life testing. Firstly, however, the ideas require TLC and kindness. The narrative around new ideas should be supportive and challenging, yes, but designed to build on the idea, not dismiss it. Getting that buy-in from others can be tricky, especially if the company's mindset (yes, mindset again) is rather brash.

TAKING ACTION

So, you now have some ideas that you're excited can solve the problem you've defined. You've analysed them and looked at them through the prism of the Four Ps (Purpose, Prowess, Potential and Profit). If all of these line up, ask, 'Why now?' Timing, I've hopefully made clear, is critical.

If one of these ideas solves a real customer problem, plays to your strengths, is sufficiently original to capture interest, and has the potential to drive growth, then it's time to test. The key question now becomes: How do I rapidly test the product in the real world and see if there is a genuine product-market fit?

The good news is that no time has been more suitable to test your product or service in the market. Rapid prototyping is widespread in all but the most niche industries, and if it's a digital service or sold digitally, then you can test ideas in a few moments. Let's make it happen.

FORGE YOUR WAY

KEY TAKEAWAYS

➡ Investing time in Originality enables new ventures to stand out in a world that is cluttered with noise.

➡ Originality takes many forms: the product is only one. Innovation doesn't have to lie in what the customer can see.

➡ Creativity is the ability to think beyond habit and conditioning. It flows best when you step away from the day-to-day and embrace diverse perspectives.

➡ Lateral thinking techniques, outlined in the FURNACE toolkit, help the creativity to keep flowing during ideation sessions.

➡ With divergent thinking complete, don't forget to come back to reality and ensure the strongest ideas are prioritised to progress into Results.

QUESTIONS TO REFLECT ON

➡ Who is involved in creating new ideas in your business? Is anyone not included?

➡ Do you give sufficient time in creating the conditions for creativity to take hold?

➡ Are all the ideas across the organisation captured consistently and placed into an ideas backlog?

➡ How could your lead ideas be strengthened by considering Doblin's ten types of innovation?

FREE RESOURCES

At www.entrepreneur-within.com/originality you'll find:

➡ Plenty of free resources to help you run creativity sessions, including a FURNACE toolkit.

➡ Templates to capture ideas, and examples of how to compile an ideas backlog.

RESULTS

SETTING SAIL

*'A ship in harbour is safe, but that
is not what ships are built for.'*

J.A. SHEDD

DIVERGENT AND CONVERGENT THINKING complete,
you're left holding a constellation of hopefully stellar ideas,
laden with passion. These ideas now need to be developed
into real products or services that can be tested with real
customers. Learning is the currency of innovation.

It is here that it all becomes very real. These ideas need
to be launched into the market so that their 'seaworthiness'
can be put to the test.

But it's all too easy for an idea to sink rather than float
because it didn't quite hit the mark in execution. So easy,
in fact, that the oft-quoted '95 per cent of new innovations
fail' (attributed to Clayton Christensen, Harvard professor
and author of the highly-acclaimed *The Innovator's
Dilemma*) is readily accepted. There are significant doubts
as to whether he ever made this claim, but the truth remains
that far more innovations fail than succeed, and those of
us with experience in innovation can reel off a list of flops
without much thought.

At this point, it's worth an aside to loop back to what
we said in Focus and the importance of clarifying the
role of innovation. Success or failure will ultimately be
determined by the ambition set at the beginning. And
while no one wants to create something that has never
been heard of, there are important cases for innovation
where the scale is small or where brand equity rather than
sales volume is the end game. The point is that success
or failure is defined by results versus expectations, and

those expectations will come back to bite if they weren't appropriately set out in the first place.

The reality is that innovation fails frequently, and the costs associated can be staggering. That could be actual monies invested, resource time or the impact on brand or corporate reputation. (Even if not always as eye-watering as the reported $170 million write-down from the Amazon Fire Phone flop that was launched in June 2014 and stopped in August 2015.)

The less measured and less reported opportunity costs are also significant. What else could have been delivered? Were eyes taken off the ball elsewhere? Did it reroute resources from elsewhere in the business?

Let's not paint too gloomy a picture, however, because the conditions have never been more favourable to launch a new venture, and the risks of failure have never been lower.

Why is that? Technology has put a world of equity, expertise and global customer responsiveness at our fingertips with relatively little investment. Entrepreneurs no longer need to risk their houses to gather the start-up capital required to test an idea, nor do corporations need to spend many thousands with agencies on market research.

It's time to reframe **Results** as less about the end game and more about a phase of discovery and optimisation. It's a phase that will enable the innovation to successfully conquer whatever sea conditions face us, and set us up for real **Growth**.

MAKING FAILURE YOUR FRIEND

'If you think that's a big failure, we're working on much bigger failures right now – and I am not kidding. Some of them are going to make the Fire Phone look like a tiny little blip.'
JEFF BEZOS

AMAZON CEO JEFF BEZOS said this in reference to the so-called innovation flop mentioned earlier. And he wasn't joking. Shareholders at Amazon have come to require a different kind of mindset towards failure and success.

So how do we best set up our environment for success, or indeed, fast failure? What's needed to truly test the hypothesis for our innovation? What are the key assumptions we need to validate? What are the reasonable timescales to assess the success or failure of a venture? What needs to change in our organisation(s) to give us the best chance of success? So many questions! Where to start? (Oops, another.)

GETTING OUT FROM BEHIND CLOSED DOORS

What so many organisations struggle with, and blue chips in particular, is the notion of 'success' being iterative. There's so often a mentality which dictates that great ideas should magically leap from development to instant success. As a result – notwithstanding the best cutting-edge research techniques – concepts are shaped internally and developed behind closed doors. They are based on models and assumed behaviour before being launched as a fait accompli and expected to deliver instant results. (Let's remind ourselves of Alan W. Watts' quote: "Instant coffee is a well-deserved punishment for being in a hurry to reach the future.")

The reality is that success, particularly sustainable success, is more often nurtured through an extended period of test and learn, of trying to figure it out. This process allows dissenting voices to be heard and listened to, enabling tweaks, add-ons or even an all-out pivot.

Clearly, there are times when commercially sensitive innovation needs to be kept under wraps and when first-mover advantage is too important in a fiercely competitive market. But typically, innovation teams overestimate these risks and underestimate the benefits of gaining – and acting on – real results at speed.

Ironically, it's often the fear of failure that keeps projects behind closed doors. This desire for perfection keeps ideas in the planning phase and away from customers for far too long, driving up costs and driving down the likelihood of subsequent in-market success. Not to mention that after so long in the development black box, there's a good chance that customers will have moved on or competitors have moved in!

DARE TO FAIL FAST; DARE TO FAIL CHEAPLY

The wholehearted acceptance – indeed embracing – of failure is key. Freedom to fail is a critical ingredient of success. In a similar vein to Amazon, the Tata Group has a 'Dare to Try' award that celebrates intelligent failure. It's based on the belief that successful innovation is often built on failure. Tata points out, 'The fact that participation in this category has increased by one hundred-fold indicates that the culture of innovation is taking root at Tata Group.'

This matters because innovation results are typically subject to a power law,[8] whereby a small percentage of ideas will produce a large percentage of the returns. If companies aren't truly comfortable enough with failure, they are unlikely to have enough bets in play to deliver outsized returns. You have to be bold enough to get the big payoffs. A 10 per cent chance to earn a 100-fold return is better than a 60 per cent chance to get a 3-fold return. For example, 10 bets with a 10 per cent chance of a 100× return with a £1m budget is a £100m return. Ten bets with a 60 per cent chance of a three-fold return with a £1m budget is just £18m. The message: go for multiple big innovation bets.

Spotify executives even measure a 'mistake rate' to ensure the company isn't being too conservative. Before launching any new innovation, it's worth considering the probability of failure. It should also be added that large companies often have a non-obvious advantage in their smaller brands. These can become perfect platforms to test early ideas. There's fear of failure that might hurt the reputation of big brands, so why not test with a smaller 'less important' brand? They are great platforms for learning.

It's not just a numbers game either; failures themselves can help to unlock the very best ideas for the future. A commonly cited example was with World War Two fighter planes. Someone decided to examine the planes that came back and decided to reinforce the places with the most bullet holes. But these were the planes that returned home. So instead, someone flipped the thinking on its head and reinforced the areas that weren't riddled with bulletholes on the planes that returned. The assumption that those which were blasted out of the sky were being hit elsewhere. It proved the correct assumption.

So, if you are going to succeed, you're going to overcome some failures along the way. If failure is likely, make sure you fail fast, and while you're at it, fail cheaply. Stop investing too much time and money secretly shaping the 'next big thing' before real customers get involved. Launch that minimal viable product; get it out there. And make a virtue of failure. Learn from Spotify, Tata and Amazon. These companies are successful because they take risks.

RESULTS IN ACTION

This idea of a Results phase being iterative is, of course, all well in theory but hard to put into practice. Larger organisations, in particular, are built to deliver shareholder returns, and they typically have a strong aversion to letting ideas 'out of the bag' too soon.

Reframing Results as a natural part of the innovation process will yield a much greater chance of sustained and profitable growth. To do this, you need to lay down the strategic foundations necessary for this approach.

Over the years, I've honed a process that helps us frame getting those results and keeps us focused on the outcome. The beauty of it is that it is circular. One of the main messages of this book is to keep innovating. This Results flow (which, incidentally, all begin with an E) encourages us to get moving, experiment, evaluate the results and then evolve the proposition with the next iteration.

So why the graphic with the archery target? Well, let's run through this analogy to think about Results. Fire the arrow and get your idea out there. That's the initial Execute step. Next, is the Experiment step. Try a bit higher? Maybe more power? Then Evaluate: have any arrows hit the bullseye, the very centre of Desirability, Viability and Feasibility? If so, hit boost and turn to the Growth chapter! If not, Evolve: how would you fire the arrow differently?

Now, if I was trying to create an easy-to-remember model, I may call these the 'Four Es of Results', or I'd play further on the arrow metaphor. In fact, I was going to, until I learned that an archery target is actually called a 'butt', and no one wants to be the author of a model called the Results Butt. Anyhoo, you get the idea: this is a cycle. Put the idea in, Execute, Experiment, Evaluate and Evolve. The best ideas will eventually move into growth.

TALES, TRAPS AND TIPS
COLIN GREENE

Colin Greene has spent 30 years working in senior leadership in technology and digital retail, including 13 years at Apple. Colin now advises scale-up tech businesses and is a Partner at Praetura Ventures.

ON SUCCESSFULLY GROWING INNOVATION

At Apple, we grew by multiplying the products. Apple would define and create a new product category, and then add another one. But Apple didn't feel the need to create a new organisation for that product; the existing team were expected to launch and execute. Even though the complexity of the product set had multiplied, the complexity of the organisation didn't. It never felt like you were working for a large enterprise.

ON CREATING SPACE FOR PEOPLE

Ideas have to come from people. You need to create an environment for people to have ideas, and create space for those people who have a left-field way of solving a problem, or coming up with something that hasn't existed before. And then you have to come up with the best execution of this incredible idea and hope the market buys into that. And if it doesn't, that's okay because you have other ideas.

ON GETTING THE TIMING RIGHT

You get your window of opportunity, and that's the genius. It's not only coming up with the idea but also the judgement and the timing around the execution of it.

ON FOCUS AND SAYING NO

It's not about throwing mud at the wall and seeing what sticks, but it's a case of coming up with a small number of ideas, recognising that you've only got so much time, and using your judgement to pick the ones you want to focus on. At Apple, we used to say there were a thousand 'nos' for every 'yes'. If you don't do that, you end up stealing time and resources away from the great ideas. The difference between a great idea and a good one can be subtle, but the best people can spot that; that was the case with Steve Jobs and the case with Tim Cook.

ON FAILING FAST

At Apple, there are tons of examples of failing fast, where leaders haven't been frightened to stop doing something if it's not working. You don't have to make a meal about that. You don't have to tell the world. A classic example would be the iPhone 5c. It was brightly coloured, with bright pink, bright yellow and bright blue options; and it was an absolute, dismal failure. People's egos did not get in the way of accepting that this didn't work. What's important is that we don't try to convince ourselves something works when it doesn't.

ON MINING A SEAM OF OPPORTUNITY

When you've found that seam of opportunity, mine it for as much as you possibly can. Look at the adjacent opportunities that you can take advantage of, but don't go so far that you stray from what's working.

ON THE LEADERSHIP FOR INNOVATION

CEOs will say they want innovation in their organisation, but are they really prepared for it? How far are they prepared to let things fail, and how much resource are they prepared to commit in the pursuit of finding the great idea? Some CEOs may talk a good game, but you find out fairly quickly after two projects are unsuccessful in a row, and they're not brave enough to go again.

ON THE BIGGEST TRAP

The biggest trap is knowing when to stop and realising when something hasn't worked out. If it hasn't been successful, call it and move on to the next thing. It's vanity to say, 'It just needs more work.' Sometimes, that is the case, but it often throws good resources after bad.

EXECUTE: *FIRE THE ARROW*

While we should accept that failure is the most likely option, there are plenty of success stories to take comfort in. If you listen carefully to those stories, though, you'll typically hear much about how the new venture learned from market feedback and mini-failures and changed tack many times before experiencing success.

If you're approaching this as a tech-led innovator or looking at innovation in marketing communications, for example, it will feel entirely achievable to get the product out in the world quickly. The digital world is perfectly placed to enable launch, learning and iteration at pace. In four words: get on with it.

On the other hand, if you're sat in a manufacturing-led business, then, given that we're really talking about rapid prototyping, your burning question is more: 'How do I deliver multiple, small-scale bets and iterate, given my manufacturing capability and constraints?'

It would be disingenuous to pretend that there is an easy answer to this, but there are a number of key strategies that, individually or combined, can help:

DEVELOP PARTNERSHIP OPPORTUNITIES

The power of partnerships is so powerful that a whole chapter (**Ecosystem**) is dedicated to them. But they have just as much relevance here in the early results phase as they do later on in growth escalation.

It's too easy for larger companies to silo themselves and assume that the answer lies within. However, when it comes to rapid prototyping, looking externally can provide a massive delivery advantage.

Co-manufacturing and co-packing might be required at the start, for example, and there is a wealth of routes available from existing suppliers, including start-ups, universities, retailers and wholesalers, who could all support and potentially strengthen delivery and speed.

'A good plan violently executed now is better than a perfect plan executed next week.'
GENERAL GEORGE S. PATTON

FIND CREATIVE ROUTES TO MARKET FOR SPEEDIER RESULTS

If a national rollout is neither desirable nor feasible, look at the ways to deliver to a limited market, whether that could be an individual retailer, region, limited-edition timeframe, specific audience and so on.

Becoming a larger brand to a smaller group of customers is very helpful for getting high-quality feedback quickly; it increases speed. It's much better to find traction with a smaller group of customers, for whom this is a large problem, than to spread yourself too thinly in the early days.

It might even be a completely different route to market than the core business, such as a university campus for a youth-targeted product or leveraging supplier networks for a below-the-radar launch. What matters is that the test market provides robust, measurable data that can be quickly accessed and actioned.

FAKE IT TILL YOU MAKE IT

There really has never been a better time to test new products in the market. Ever. Buy ads on Google against search terms and see if people click. Set up a new product or even a new website and discover what people add to the basket. You don't even need a product; just set up a 'Sorry, we're out of stock' banner. You will, however, have a very good idea if people are interested.

EXPERIMENT: FIRE MORE ARROWS!

It's tempting to only fire one arrow before evaluating. The trouble with this is that it can slow down the pace of learning. If you can, get multiple bets out there. The ideas we do get out into the market should also never be static. They should constantly be improved through iteration and experimentation. It's fanciful to believe that an idea will be fully formed on its first outing. Do not let the quest for perfection get in the way of progress. Embrace imperfection. Then iterate like mad!

'I have not failed. I've just found 10,000 ways that won't work.'
THOMAS EDISON

TALES, TRAPS AND TIPS
IAN BENTON

Ian Benton is a CEO, founder, and brand marketer. He launched and built brands at Nestlé and Coca-Cola before launching his own bedding business in France. He now helps small and medium businesses become more focused, organised, efficient, and profitable.

ON TESTING INNOVATION

Large companies could test innovation much better. Small businesses are much better at getting rapid customer validation. Remember the famous Innocent smoothie example, where they made a few smoothies in the kitchen and went to sell them at a market. They had two buckets saying: 'Should we launch this as a brand or not? Yes or no.' Big companies miss that step and rely far too heavily on market research.

ON CHECKING THERE IS REAL DEMAND

The first question is always to check that there is a genuine customer need, rather than this being a great idea that's looking for a problem. This has to be done before you've got to the point where you've designed a website and taken the product photos. If it's a drinks brand, I'd make 500 samples and create a pop-up stall as close as possible to your target market, such as a festival or football ground. Think how you can test your ideas rapidly, but for as low a cost as possible? So you're not making too significant bets too early.

ON WHY YOU SHOULD LISTEN TO YOUR SALES TEAM

Always discuss innovation with the sales team. Don't limit your conversations to the marketing team. The sales people will go out there and get the distribution and hear first hand what customers think. Sales teams have a wealth of experience in big businesses. So how can you use that sales team and say, do we think we should launch this? Yes or no? It's amazing how siloed some organisations are.

And I mean it. There is a theory called Boyd's Law,[9] which I wholeheartedly believe in. It states that the speed of iteration beats the quality of iteration. Make small and fast changes and get rid of what's not working. The speed of the changes, however, very much depends on the sector and the amount of data required to draw meaningful conclusions. Those used to working in an agile environment will already be set up for this speed of change.

One excellent example is Booking.com. Many companies invest substantial sums in A/B testing and multi-variant testing programmes. Booking.com started using this approach in 2005, and according to Christophe Perrin, Group Product Manager at Booking.com, it has 'scaled and democratised experimentation to the point where today most product changes across all of Booking.com are first exposed to end-users through our experimentation platform'. Like all companies involved with experimentation, Booking.com are interested in ensuring – and measuring – whether the decisions taken on the back of these experiments are based on reliable evidence and whether these decisions support the values and objectives of the company. Booking.com fire a lot of arrows... as you'll have noticed from the last time you booked a hotel room through the site.

There are two practical tips to learn from here when experimenting:

➡ First, be clear on your hypothesis at the start. Write it down and sense-check it against the outcome of Focus. Does it support advancing the Four Ps of Purpose, Prowess, Potential and Profit?

➡ Secondly, write down the evaluation metrics before the experiment begins. It's incredible how many times the proposed evaluation metrics change as the experiment progresses, seemingly to support 'new insight' but typically as the result of emotional sponsorship for the well-liked concepts of senior leadership. We'll dive further into this next.

Anyone involved in innovation must appreciate that there will always be multiple ways of solving their chosen problem. (Those arrows to labour the point.) The trick lies in discovering which one of the many solutions offers the most potential. Remember, don't fall in love with the solution.

Instead of launching 'the one', it can be more helpful to place multiple low-cost bets. The purpose of these bets is to learn, test the riskiest hypotheses, and hope at least one materialises into a bet that's worth developing. As soon as one shows promise, resources are invested in accelerating momentum and learning. Those without traction have the funding withdrawn but always carry the insights forward.

It is an ethos we carried through at Beer Hawk. There were four core values. The two that really chime here, when taken together, were 'We get on with it' and 'We always make it better'. Being true to these values forced us to get things done, to launch things before we were truly ready. We embraced the fact that we would not get it entirely right the first time around. Crucially, we were also ready to get an improved v2 out quickly, a v3, and so on until we'd found something that resonated. Or until we'd realised the need to move on to something else.

The principle here is about prioritising progress over perfection, recognising that it's highly unlikely any one bet will be fully formed at its first outing. Be prepared to embrace imperfection, get it out there 80 per cent right, and then iterate, iterate, iterate. Remember, we're talking here about a minimal viable product; it may not be perfect, but it still needs to genuinely function and solve the problem.

And also, in many organisations, how often are the 'failures' or the 'not quite successes' even acknowledged, let alone celebrated? The faster you embrace failure, the faster you are likely to celebrate success.

EVALUATE: HAVE WE
HIT THE BULLSEYE?

Once the multiple bets are in the market and the experiments are set, it's time to evaluate those metrics that truly matter. At this point, we need to clarify exactly what we mean by measurement and what needs to be measured. Businesses can so frequently get hung up on the wrong measurements or don't measure in a way that allows for speedy optimisation. With advances in technology, there are not only more data points that could be monitored than ever before, but there's also been a corresponding increase in computing power, machine learning and data visualisation to help make sense of it.

Being clear on the success metrics and decision-making process can greatly increase the speed of iteration. But what are those success metrics? Let's start by distinguishing between lead and lag indicators.

LAG VERSUS LEAD INDICATORS

Very simply put, lag indicators measure the outcome. Did we achieve the intended result? Examples of lag indicators include sales volume, profit or market share. Lead indicators measure things that show progress towards the goal. Lead indicators attempt to predict future outcomes and offer information we can act on. Glance down at the Robert Louis Stevenson quote below. The seeds you plant today are the lead indicators, and the harvest is the lag indicator.

Both types of indicators can be useful, but for a new innovation venture, it tends to be more helpful to concentrate on lead indicators. We're looking forward. Like driving a car, we're looking at signposts, we're watching obstacles, and constantly taking on new information that informs how we drive. We can't drive forwards when only looking through the rear-view mirror. You're much more likely to achieve the desired outcomes – lag indicators – if you consider the right combination of lead indicators.

A great example is the Facebook 'aha moment' when

'Do not measure success by today's harvest. Measure success by the seeds you plant today.'
ROBERT LOUIS STEVENSON

they recognised that their focus needed to be not on the huge-scale targets but on the smallest level of customer behaviour. Chamath Palihapitiya, then VP of User Growth, said: 'After all the testing, all the iterating, all of this stuff, you know what the single biggest thing we realised? Get any individual to seven friends in ten days. That was it. Do you want a keystone? That was our keystone. There's not much more complexity than that.'

Before we move on I do want to plant a word of warning here. It's all too easy to read increases and decreases in metrics that are actually a natural variation. Did you have an amazing weekend selling beer simply because it was warm outside, or there was a big football game on? Sometimes, it's appropriate to use statistical tools to help identify when a metric breaks out of a normal pattern rather than the noise of normal variation.

THE HOLY TRINITY OF METRICS

The choice of specific metrics is vast and will naturally depend on the nature of the innovation, test market, data capability, and so forth. I have found the Desirability, Viability, Feasibility (DVF) framework to be the most useful way to identify the high-level questions that Results ultimately need to answer. This DVF trifecta originated from IDEO[10] in the early 2000s and seeks to validate three fundamental hypotheses:

→ **Desirability.** Do customers want it? Is the proposed solution desirable? Is it a solution that your customers really need? Is your new innovation idea a painkiller or a vitamin? Painkillers, by definition, solve an immediate pain and, therefore, tend to be bought as soon as a customer becomes aware of the 'pain'. Vitamins, on the other hand, are helpful and things that should be bought, but the urgency isn't there to make an immediate purchase decision.

→ **Viability.** Does it make money? Is there evidence to suggest that the business model will be sustainable? How do customers want to pay for this solution, and does this fit with our business reality? If not, what has to be true for our business model to work? Does our solution also contribute to the long-term purpose of the business, including any sustainability commitments?

➡ **Feasibility.** Can we build it? Can we deliver the promise of the value proposition? Going further, does it build on your prowess and existing capabilities? If a solution requires building entirely new capabilities, then this innovation becomes riskier. Is the functionality required possible today, or will it be possible in the future?

Hitting the DVF metrics in the bullseye won't happen often. When they do, you hit Boost (see below) and move on to scaling your venture, which is what the Growth chapter deals with. If not, we move on to Evolve (see below). This allows us to re-aim the trajectory, the speed, the direction of the arrow.

EVOLVE: *HOW SHALL WE FIRE THE ARROW DIFFERENTLY?*

'The one most responsive'. I want to stress those four words in this very famous quote, (right) that don't often get the significance they deserve. As a company launching a new innovation, you must be the most responsive in your market, especially at the Results stage. It's during this test-and-learn period when all your earlier assumptions are put to the test; it's the time when the most important decisions are made about the future of the whole venture.

It is helpful to consider four options for each potential solution that's in play.

➡ **Pause.** The early data isn't great. Note that this isn't stopping. It is simply halting the potential solution and moving it to the backlog, where it could be picked up again if conditions change.

➡ **Redesign.** This solution isn't working in its current form, but there is something to learn from. With some (maybe fundamental) changes, this idea has the potential to continue. Let's go back to move forwards.

'It is not the strongest of the species that survive, nor the most intelligent, but the one most responsive to change.'

CHARLES DARWIN

TALES, TRAPS AND TIPS
DIRK MISCHENDAHL

Dirk Mischendahl is a serial entrepreneur. He founded Northern Bloc Ice Cream, a plant-based ice cream company and previously started a hugely successful communications agency. He enjoys all things food and drink.

ON KEEPING THE FOCUS NARROW

I think focus is the hardest thing. At Northern Bloc, we set out to be as innovative as possible, a sustainable ice cream company that was doing it differently. We were spinning off all these ideas, but you just lose focus. You're doing everything a little bit rubbish. You don't have the resources; you don't have the money. Really, we should have said, 'Right, pick one or two.'

ON KNOWING YOUR CUSTOMERS

The thing that shocked me the most in our growth phase was that we thought we were brilliant on social media. We were always so ahead of the game. We were growing followers and doing really well. Then we did the shopper analysis and looked at who was really buying our stuff in retail, and the shoppers were nothing like our social media followers. I realised that whilst we'd built up a great following, it wasn't making us any money!

ON FAILURE

I think the word failure in itself is a bad word. I don't see things as failing; I see things as new beginnings. I know that sounds corny, but you have to ask: what did we learn from it? How does that help to take us to the next place?

ON TESTING DESIRABILITY WHILE MAKING MONEY

You have to do the costings and demand modelling simultaneously. After proving desirability, commercial viability is the most important. If it's not making money, cut it quickly.

- ➡ **Play.** Continue to experiment and learn about this potential solution. It might be too early to have sufficient data to draw conclusions, but the evidence suggests there is something to work with. Keep the testing going.
- ➡ **Boost.** The early data suggest that this potential solution is likely to work and could become the next big thing. It's time to give it more resources and exposure to accelerate learning and evolution. This is the pathway to Growth.

Results is a dynamic phase of continued learning and improvement. Patience matters, especially in a corporate world of instant results and high expectations.

So what happens if we decide to pull the plug on the innovation or innovations we have out there because they just aren't gaining traction? Well, it's back to the ideas we progressed during Originality. We start the Four Es again: Execute, Experiment, Evaluate... and Evolve. We may even have to go back to Focus. Consider again the problem we're trying to solve. We keep evolving until we get traction. Persevere. Lack of patience is why we have instant coffee.

And what happens when we hit the bullseye? We scale our venture carefully and sustainably – and that's all covered in the next chapter. But to be clear, the central tenet of this book is that we must continue to innovate. Put into place the mechanism that continually assesses other ideas. Keep innovating, always.

READY TO GROW

The Four Es approach has provided a framework of key considerations (Execute, Experiment, Evaluate and Evolve), but at its heart is the reframing from **Results** as the endgame to Results as part of the game.

Reimagine results as a stepping stone in which real-world validation is sought, and failure embraced, thereby setting up sustainable innovation that is ready to sail into the **Growth** phase. It tends to be easier to invalidate something than it does to validate it. We have a new

'It may seem difficult at first, but everything is difficult at first.'
MIYAMOTO MUSASHI

product or service that is desirable, viable and feasible. It's now time to change your mindset again for growth, make sure that we catch a trade wind, and speed up. But never forget that you need more ideas in your back pocket. The innovation process must always continue, making a secure, rigorous and grown-up business out of the venture that is succeeding. All that at the same time. It's about being ambidextrous, remember?

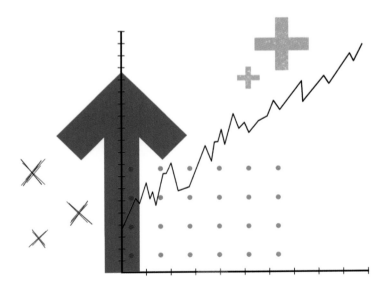

FORGE YOUR WAY

KEY TAKEAWAYS

➡ Ideas need to get out from behind closed doors quickly and be tested with real customers.

➡ Results is a phase of discovery and optimisation: execute the testing quickly, experiment, evaluate the results and then evolve the product.

➡ Seek out the leading indicators to prove (or disprove) Desirability, Viability and Feasibility.

➡ Failure must be embraced and not feared. Dare to fail fast; dare to fail cheaply. And celebrate it.

➡ Think of Results as a stepping stone, not the end game. It's a continuous innovation loop.

QUESTIONS TO REFLECT ON

➡ How quickly can you move from having an idea to having a prototype in the market and getting real results?

➡ When was the last time you failed? What did you learn? Are you failing frequently enough?

➡ Are you monitoring the right lead indicators to cover Desirability, Viability and Feasibility?

➡ Do you have enough tests live in the market right now?

FREE RESOURCES

At www.entrepreneur-within.com/results you'll find:

➡ Videos and articles designed to help you progress through the innovation testing cycle.

➡ Downloadable templates to support DVF testing, and examples of Lead vs Lag metrics.

GROWTH

REACHING ESCAPE VELOCITY

'Timing, perseverance, and ten years of trying will eventually make you look like an overnight success.'

BIZ STONE, CO-FOUNDER OF TWITTER

REACH FOR THE STARS

Escape velocity. It's the moment in celestial mechanics when an object reaches the velocity to escape gravitational pull and launches itself into new territory. If it doesn't achieve this velocity, it becomes stuck in an orbit or, worse, comes crashing back down.

Most new business ventures don't reach escape velocity, the moment when it reaches product-market fit, when demand takes on a life of its own. Most launches get stuck at a certain turnover and are unable to break out. That might be OK for some, but as we saw in Part One, if you're not growing, you're dying. If the business is stable, it's eventually going to be overtaken by a competitor.

Within large corporations, it's more acute. If the new venture isn't making money and quickly, it often isn't given the chance to reach escape velocity. I've seen it with new beer brands, soft drinks and beauty care products. Some launches are able to ignite, develop rapidly and reach significance as a brand or business that can stand on its own. Other ventures just manage to stay in orbit, struggle to find growth and eventually spiral down into insignificance. We've all seen those that plummet despite showing initial promise.

If you've experienced initial traction, it's time to turn the afterburners on and scale. Scaling a new venture is hard, but the point of this chapter is to offer practical guidance that makes the scale-up journey a little easier.

HIGH GROWTH IS FOR
THE FEW, NOT THE MANY

When results do show traction, you'd imagine that scaling follows naturally. But what does 'scaling' actually mean? How achievable is it? And how do we tip the odds so they are in our favour?

The reality is that the vast majority of ventures are not built to scale and reach escape velocity. Given the disproportionate coverage of the most successful innovations and businesses, it's easy to assume that scaling up is relatively straightforward and commonplace.

Much has been written in recent years about 'unicorns', those businesses which reach a valuation of over £1 billion, yet statistics show that a start-up has an approximately 0.00006 per cent probability of joining this esteemed club. Even acknowledging that £1 billion is way beyond the scope or ambitions of most new ventures, we define 'scale-ups' as businesses that have successfully broken out of start-up mode. According to the Office for National Statistics (ONS), these businesses account for 0.6 per cent of UK Small and Medium Enterprises (SMEs).

The same is also true for innovation within larger organisations. As discussed in the **Results** chapter, big corporations typically struggle with getting ideas off the ground in the first place. They are not set up financially, logistically or culturally to embrace the entrepreneurial mindset required to gain traction. Their scale-up challenges are even more pronounced as they battle to grow something that has probably had insufficient real-market incubation. They are, in effect, attempting to amalgamate **Results** and **Growth** in order to accelerate up the curve much too soon and much too fast, leading – unsurprisingly – to very little scale-up success.

Why is this? What is getting in the way? Regardless of the size of the organisation, the barriers to growth for new ventures are remarkably similar.

START-UP VS CORPORATE GROWTH

	START-UP INNOVATION	CORPORATE INNOVATION
AMBITION	Many entrepreneurs aren't looking to scale up. They could be building a lifestyle business. But ambition requires role models who have scaled successfully.	Big businesses tend to get ambitions the wrong way around: too big in the short term, too small in the long term, limiting growth from the outset.
FINANCE	Growth capital is perceived as a key barrier when data suggests it's, in fact, a much smaller issue. Cash flow is often the more immediate issue for most start-ups.	The business model is often a major stumbling block for innovation in corporations. Achieving the right margin – at scale – is often both critical and impossible in the short term.
TALENT & EXPERTISE	It's difficult to compete with salaries, benefits and career progression that big businesses can offer. Limited budget means that SMEs rely on enthusiasm more than expertise.	Big businesses have no shortage of talent and expertise; their challenge is channelling that talent in the right direction. The 'best' employees gravitate to the biggest roles.
NETWORKS & ECOSYSTEMS	Opportunities for new markets, contracts and joint ventures typically materialise from connections and networks. This Ecosystem is hard to nurture when it's all hands on deck.	In theory, big businesses should be able to leverage networks with ease. But often larger businesses tend to assume that capability is already within, rather than reaching out to partners and connections.

To cut to the chase, scaling up – by which we really mean sustainable scaling up – is damn hard. It's also slow.

High-profile innovations, brands and businesses can often look as though they've just exploded into the market when the truth is that they have a 'silent tail' comprising years of 'test and learn' and slow growth.

Add to hard and slow: non-linear. There are plenty of examples of businesses that have got off to a great start only to falter and, in some cases, forced to pivot or even stop.

According to a report by PitchBook, out of all the start-ups that have successfully built a product, become reasonably well-established and completed at least series B funding, only 22 per cent succeed independently at getting to series C funding. In other words, they set off well; investors saw the potential, but they somehow failed to translate that into the scaleable growth required to unlock the next level of capital.

All of this sounds pretty demoralising and may make you wonder why you'd want to bother at all. And yet, when innovations do succeed, when they do make it big, they matter. They drive value, and they change how we behave.

According to the ScaleUp Institute 2022 Annual Review, the 0.6 per cent of UK SMEs that could be classed as scale-ups contributed £1.2 trillion to the UK economy at the end of 2022. Yet, they employed more than three million people. Not to mention the impact of consumer and shopper behaviour. Growth champions indeed.

We're talking about start-up statistics here because there are many more statistics about start-up and scale-up ventures than ventures within larger organisations. Corporations are, understandably, sheepish about giving stats on those innovations that failed. But the fundamental trajectory is comparable.

It's in the interest of economies and organisations to want more of these scale-up ventures and to do that, we need to understand what it really takes to overcome these growth barriers.

TALES, TRAPS AND TIPS
ANDY LOGAN

Andy Logan is Vice President, PerfectDraft at Anheuser-Busch InBev. Previously he has been in charge of global e-commerce and worked on brands such as Stella Artois.

ON FINDING THE RIGHT PROBLEM

One of the most common mistakes is investing too little time in finding the right problem. There are at least three layers to this. First, you need to deeply understand the problem itself. Then you need to discern whether the problem is a 'vitamin' or a 'painkiller'. Is it nice to solve or critical to solve? And therefore how material is the addressable market? Finally, there is real magic in finding a problem that you intrinsically care about solving. Falling in love with the problem in this way is at the very heart of whether you'll be able to deliver a great solution that can scale into a meaningful business.

ON PLACING MULTIPLE BETS

We were actively trialling lots of potential solutions because we knew many of them wouldn't work. It wasn't just about the solutions themselves; we needed to establish an iterative loop for testing the problems. If a solution got traction quickly, that would help us validate and learn more about the problem. We'd look at how big the addressable market was and then decide whether we should prioritise or kill it and move on.

ON DISPROVING A HYPOTHESIS

It's much easier to invalidate something than to validate it. I try as hard as I can to disprove a hypothesis. And if I can't, I accept it as true and keep going.

ON ZERO TO ONE AND THEN ONE TO ONE HUNDRED

Through experiences of successful and unsuccessful graduations of ventures from our incubator to the core business, we learnt that in order to successfully scale ventures, we needed three phases, 0–1, 1–10 and finally 10–100.

Zero to one was about falling in love with the problem and finding a solution. One to ten was when we had confirmed that solving the problem would meaningfully contribute to the central corporate strategy and that we had a validated solution. The solution needed to be 10 times better than any other available, utilise the mothership to create a competitive advantage and be scaleable to a level that could enhance the wider company's ability to deliver its strategy. During this phase, we readied the venture for integration.

Ten to one hundred is about actually scaling the solution by integrating it into the mothership's core management system. It is triggered at the point the solution becomes of such scale and relevance that it is captured as a priority in the core business's long-term plan. Moving from 10 to 100 feels radically different because you transition from a people-led approach to a process-led approach.

ON A POTENTIAL BLIND SPOT

It is very tough to find people who can both innovate and operate at scale. I find it more helpful to think about the different horizons for innovation. You need fantastic people to operate at scale and others thinking more laterally to build the future. Naturally, the senior leadership of an organisation tends to be populated by those who have been successful in operating at scale. This can create a blindspot when it comes to championing more radical ideas, which is something a great leader needs to stay constantly aware of.

WHAT GOT US HERE
WILL NOT TAKE US THERE

'Only those who will risk going too far can possibly find out how far one can go.'
T.S. ELIOT

BEYOND THE VERY PRACTICAL BARRIERS that we've highlighted above, the single biggest barrier to scaling up is often that mindset does not shift as fast as growth opportunities. All the passion, all the focus, the speed, and even the early customers that got you out of the starting blocks, will not be enough to keep the momentum going. They could even slow you down. Any innovation needs to be dynamic and flexible, and these principles also apply to mindsets and ways of working when scaling.

The second shift in mindset is embracing some big business rigour. While these are short points, they are fundamental to the success and sustainability of the venture.

THE MOVING-ON MINDSET

Given the sweat and tears that went into starting the new venture, it's very easy for an innovator to believe the business model and assumptions in the business plan are the best they can be. And why not, after all that work to find the right problem with Focus, developing distinctive ideas with Originality, and experimenting to unlock early Results? Things might be going well and the thought of making new and different choices can feel, at best, daunting, and at worst, foolhardy.

While running Beer Hawk, I sat down with my coach to envision what it would be like at £40 million in revenue. It felt ridiculous at the time. We were so far from £40 million.

In fact, we hadn't yet reached £10 million. But we visualised it in incredible detail. What people would be in the business? How would we communicate? What would our product offering look like? What new customers would we be attracting? How would our fulfilment operations work?

The breakthrough insight was the need to attract a new type of customer. Our initial target of 'Beer Connoisseurs', wonderfully engaged and engaging people who might fondly be referred to as beer geeks, was simply not big enough to quadruple the business. The concern was that by going more mainstream – in the quest for scale – we risked alienating the very people upon whom our fledgling business had relied. In fact, without realising, the change had already started. Without deliberately setting out to become a gift destination, we had nevertheless naturally attracted another segment of people we called 'Inventive Gifters', as well as a less discerning but significantly larger segment of 'Beer Explorers'.

Actively positioning the brand towards these broader groups felt uncomfortable. It watered down our credibility with the original fan base but, crucially, introduced hundreds of thousands of new customers to the wonderful world of craft beer. And that was the growth required to ultimately scale the business tenfold. We envisioned the change needed and acted as though the business had already reached our £40 million stretch target.

We would not have achieved scale had we not changed our mindset. There's no pretending that this is an easy transition and some of our earliest employees left the business as a result. But we had the ambition to scale rapidly and we needed to change our outlook accordingly.

This moving-on mindset is equally applicable to a founder within an organisation. In all likelihood, the founder will be naturally better at starting than scaling, I certainly was. We needed to strengthen our management team to bring in capabilities that we didn't have as founders. We simply couldn't have done it without them.

'Growth is never by mere chance; it is the result of forces working together.'
JAMES CASH PENNEY

SCALING-UP RIGOUR

The other aspect of this mental shift is bringing new rigour to ways of working.

The early stages of innovation are, by necessity, defined by creativity and fluidity. Even when applying the best strategic thinking and planning, it's an all-hands-on-deck, fly-by-the-seat-of-your-pants period. It's a style that brings enormous energy and allows for all of the behaviours that we discussed in **Originality** and **Results** to really flourish. Indeed, for many entrepreneurs or intrapreneurs, this is exactly the way of working that suits their personalities and on which they thrive.

The problem is that start-up ways of working are not suited to scaling up. It's physically and mentally impossible for everyone to do everything. The growing size of the venture demands a growing team and new processes. The increasing number of decision-makers requires more formal communication, as well as reliability and predictability. Not everything can go through the founders.

Thinking like a scale-up is one thing, but you need to act like one by actively, explicitly, and consistently applying the rigour that a bigger business demands. This is likely to involve strengthening the squad.

TALES, TRAPS AND TIPS
IRENE GRAHAM

Irene Graham OBE is the founding CEO of the ScaleUp Institute, which is dedicated to ensuring that the UK is the best place in the world not just to start, but to scale a business.

ON THE DIFFICULTIES OF SCALING IN THE UK

We found several issues that the UK faced compared to other countries ahead of us in scaling up. One was the depth of capital across the UK in terms of funding for a scale-up journey, whether that be institutional capital or sovereign wealth funds. This is an area the current government is focused on addressing through the British Business Bank; British Growth Partnership; National Wealth Fund and pension fund reforms.

ON THE IMPORTANCE OF LOCAL ECOSYSTEMS IN SCALING

We know the drivers for local growth, such as access to skilled talent, access to clusters, access to growth capital, and also how the university anchors work together. So, our big focus at the ScaleUp Institute has been working with local and regional ecosystems from the start. We've got really great businesses that are now growing, but we still need to make sure we're connecting them to the markets, the people and the money, hence the ScaleUp Britain campaign focus.

ON MAINTAINING FOCUS

You can have so many opportunities coming towards you. One of the most important things is to keep focused on what you know and what you're good at. Look at how you build that.

ON GETTING THE RIGHT ADVISERS

Really do think about the peer network around you, and the group of mentors or advisers, or indeed, what your board structure is: Have you got the right mix of people to help you in that growth journey? Have we got the ingredients within our leadership for growth?

STRENGTHENING THE SQUAD –
MY BEER HAWK EXPERIENCE

MY OWN EXPERIENCE SAW 'two mates in a shed' become a team of more than 200 within 10 years. That pace of growth certainly sets no records, but we experienced first-hand the constant challenges of team evolution, recruitment, retention and reorganisation. Like most scale-up businesses, we made frequent mistakes along the way. I'd managed large teams before, but the experience of rapid people growth was something new.

At the start, it was all deceptively simple. We needed help with packing and order processing. We prioritised attitude and work ethic, as we knew that we could teach people what to do. We struck gold with two individuals who actively made it a better place to be. With such a small team – and in a pretty small space – they naturally got involved in conversations about the future. Everyone knew everything, and we relished the energy and camaraderie of such a tight-knit team. But when we reached eight employees, the dynamic began to shift.

We had recruited to our values, but as the business grew, necessity also drove us to seek more specific skills and experiences. It became clear that some people were better at talking about future direction and strategy than others; some people preferred to stay within what they knew, and others were keen to develop themselves. And with a bigger team, it simply wasn't practical or feasible to have everyone involved in everything any more. It was a natural progression. But as we created our first 'inner circle', by default, it meant that some people were no longer in it.

Yes, there were teething troubles, and we had to work incredibly hard to forge an inclusive and energised culture, but you cannot run a strategic democracy. As we grew beyond twenty people, it made sense to formalise a structure with a leadership team and our first organisational hierarchy (*shudder). We held on to some of our early employees, and others dropped off, but by applying more rigour to the organisation, we could always keep a close eye on the health of the company culture, which was critical to our ongoing growth.

As we continued to grow, we noticed that at certain stages of team growth, the culture changed, slightly at first and then significantly. I call this my scaling rule of 2.5. That's to say, every time our team grew by a factor of roughly 2.5, there was a noticeable shift in culture. At 20, some 'originals' started to work for people who were not the founders. At 50 people, we needed to instigate monthly 'town hall' meetings. At 125, it became very different again. I learned that you need to be prepared for reaching these milestones in the way you communicate, in the way you make decisions and in the way you deal with people. And you need to do it before you reach that number. This rule of 2.5 is something that seems to reasonate with other entrepreneurs I've spoken to. Be aware that this is a thing. Get ahead of it.

To help the venture founder scale and embrace this mindset and different ways of working, it helps to be surrounded by a supportive group focused on assisting the venture reach escape velocity.

REACHING ESCAPE VELOCITY

*'If I have seen further,
it is by standing on the
shoulders of giants.'*
ISAAC NEWTON

THINKING AND ACTING LIKE A SCALE-UP is a great
intention, but it is much harder to put into practice when
there is a maelstrom of decisions and demands on your time
– new customers, capabilities, suppliers, team members. The
pace of change can be intoxicating, and there is often a sense
in those early days that 'all growth is good'. This is, of course,
far from the case.

Now is the time to apply a more structured approach,
both to gain perspective and to slow down in order to speed
up. So, how do you actually go about doing that?

SUPPORT, NOT SCRUTINY

When a new venture is growing, it's not just the business
that is scaling but activities, decisions, choices and an
all-around pull on a leader's time. It's stressful, and the
innovator-in-chief can frequently lose sight of the wood for
the trees. You are also marking your own homework.

To inject diligence and an invaluable dollop of objective
realism, you need to establish an external viewpoint on
the business. It needs to be external and beyond what
the executive leadership team can provide too. External
start-ups would have a board with non-executive directors
and advisors. I'm surprised by how infrequently internal
founders have something similar.

Whether you call this a 'growth board', 'advisory board'
or something else, it's important to have a mechanism

that brings regular external perspective and support. I've called this section 'Support, not scrutiny', to make clear the difference between a board that is answerable to shareholders and a group of people who will leave their job titles at the door and support you. Gently. The members of the growth board need to bring their expertise and knowledge to the table and unwaveringly support the venture. I personally prefer the term 'growth board' as it's clear to everyone what the objective is.

These growth boards don't need to be enormous, and it's important to remember that their primary purpose is to advise on strategic direction. Not to call the shots. However, they should be individuals with business credibility, a commitment to seeing the venture succeed, and the ability and willingness to support and challenge. I think the most effective growth boards include external advisors, but I've also seen this work well when comprised of an internal team from the parent company.

At PerfectDraft, the growth board meetings included some of the key members of the global company, but we made sure to lift our heads from the day-to-day.

To help make it easier to ensure we covered everything, and because we're now all about the take-off phases, I developed a model for these meetings that conveniently spells ROCKET to drive the agenda of a growth board. This covers our Reason, Organisation and Culture, as well as KPIs, Expenses and Testing. I've found it helpful to break down these meetings into two separate sections. The first three agenda points cover 'strategy and people', while the second three elements cover 'performance and projects'.

HOW TO: ROCKET

It's important to focus the agenda of these growth boards in a way that genuinely helps the leadership team of this new venture and to avoid getting bogged down in reviewing lag metrics and financial reports that don't particularly supercharge growth.

REASON WHY

Focus doesn't stop at the start-up stage. As innovation grows, it's critical to maintain a constant line of questioning over what you're trying to achieve, where you could go, and how well the current solution is meeting your ambition. It may sound counter-intuitive when you've done all of that thinking already, but the only constant is change. Market conditions, new competitors, sociocultural trends, global events, and even personal circumstances can collude to require a re-think. It's always worth checking in regularly to see why this venture exists, even if the answer is 'well, yes, it's abundantly clear'.

Now is a good time to re-read the Focus chapter or ask yourself questions, including:

➡ What's the mission and reason (why) behind this venture? How do these align with our parent company?

➡ What objectives do we need to achieve?

➡ Are we still thinking widely about the Total Addressable Problem and the underlying intent behind the problem we are solving.

➡ Do our priorities and roadmap connect with our ambition?

ORGANISATION

Scaling a new venture requires regular checks on organisational design and working methods. Whether this venture is on a path to scaling to become a stand-alone business or destined to become integrated into the parent company at some point, key decisions need to be made about how best to organise.

The venture will develop organically as capacity gaps are filled and processes become more efficient, but there comes a point when consciously developing the organisation needs to receive as much focus as building the business.

Consider three elements when developing your organisation.

The first is **capability**. It's about finding people with the skills, knowledge and expertise that you need. This will usually include growing from a new venture team of generalists to developing the key functional areas that you would typically see in a larger business. It could even entail questioning whether the people who were right to start the venture are still right to lead its growth trajectory.

The second element that needs to be considered under the banner 'Organisation' is **process**. While processes can eventually become the enemy of new ideas, it's at this growth stage that we need to enable the venture to function effectively. But don't go overboard. It's easy to fall into the corporate trap of over-processing, especially if the team comes from a corporate background. It's about just getting enough processes to ensure that the business isn't at risk of tripping up over foundational requirements and developing the muscle to scale at speed.

The final element is **systems**. And, from experience, this can often become a sticking point. Do you take advantage of, say, the existing accounting systems of the parent company or maintain your own?

Knowing the future pathway is important here, but it's worth a regular review to scan the market for new developments and optimise your tech stack where possible.

CULTURE

The number of teams who don't actively talk about this is staggering. The question of culture is emotionally charged. It's also less obviously connected to business outcomes and, therefore, easy to deprioritise. However, most business leaders attest that culture can make or break an organisation. For a venture within a large organisation, an alignment of values is immensely helpful, but everyone needs to appreciate how differences in culture can manifest themselves. Clarity of culture is key here, as much for your team as all the other ones in the business spying on your beanbags, colourful wall hangings and away days.

The challenge in scaling a venture is how to nurture a culture that came so naturally rather than easily in the start-up phase. It's easy to feel like one team chasing one goal. You're fired by a communal spirit when you're just a handful. It is far harder to keep that alive when that team has multiplied into tens and then hundreds.

Here's what you need to consider:

➡ Articulate the business values clearly for everyone, and then commit to them in practice and in plain sight. Leaders need to be seen to be 'walking the talk' and to be calling out when others do the same.

➡ Find a 'canary'. This could be anyone who is highly trusted and who really understands the values of the venture. They will provide an early warning of issues or tell them as they are.

➡ Build a high alignment and high autonomy company. Henrik Kniberg developed an Alignment Autonomy Matrix. It is simple, really. On the X-axis is autonomy, and on the Y-axis is alignment. Typically, a high-growth venture within a larger parent company will want high alignment to the company's mission, but also high autonomy, free of the shackles of big business.

KPIS

We've talked about measurement extensively, but the headline key performance indicators need to be reviewed at every growth board. You need measurable indicators of success that you and all stakeholders understand. Choosing the right KPIs is the difficult bit. Here's what to consider.

➡ You get what you measure, so choose the KPIs wisely and ruthlessly; which indicators will genuinely prove success? Which will drive real decisions?

→ It's no good having KPIs at the top without cascading them down. Everyone in the business should have personal goals that ladder directly back to the KPIs. This way, everything is done in service of the higher ambition, and everyone is responsible.

→ Build a dashboard. Create a consistent, visual and single-source performance measurement that can quickly tell the story. You need to avoid multiple versions of the truth. This should include twelve-month rolling forecasts that include explicit assumptions about the risks facing the business and the key opportunities you plan to take advantage of.

EXPENSES

Expenses are critical enough to merit their own mention because the new venture will live or die on how well the cash runway is managed. In the P&L, expenses are the only items for which you have direct control. This directly impacts the length of the cash runway.

Revenue and expenses do not tend to form a linear relationship. At the start, investments need to be made, and there are stress points to resolve, all of which require cash outlay. The venture may well be structurally unprofitable in the early phase until economies of scale kick in. All of this places enormous pressure on a new business's ability to continue scaling up or even continue at all.

The point here is to be rigorously attentive to expenses. Review regularly and, in particular, ensure clarity of current and projected burn rates. Patience is key here. If you build too quickly and therefore spend too quickly, as is a tendency within large organisations, losses can open up just as quickly.

TESTING

A high-growth venture needs to cling to the flexibility and dynamism that got it off the ground in the first place, even as it's establishing itself in the market. Be alive to the reality that the growth will eventually reach its peak. The experimentation cycle that started in Results must continue in the knowledge that there should be more tests ready to boost into the growth phase. The most innovative companies are running thousands of experiments each year. Jeff Bezos directly addresses this. "Our success is a function of how many experiments we do per year, per month, per week, per day."

Testing in the growth phase should look like this:

➡ Never stop iterating, and always make it better. Renovation will attract new customers and re-attract those who may have drifted. However, you need to be aware of knee-jerk reactions to customer feedback and 'over-customising' for the sake of it.

➡ Watch intently outside your organisation. Keep an eye on the market, eye up the customers, stay on top of the wider socio-cultural-tech trends to build a sense of the future. How are your competitors experimenting? Are they measuring, and celebrating, the failure rate?

➡ Every lead campaign should be challenged. As a rule of thumb for marketing campaigns, keep 80 per cent of your budget behind the champion (best performing) campaign. Then 20 per cent of your budget should be used on a challenger campaign to see if it can outperform. Multiple challengers-in-waiting should be developed to ensure a constant flow of champion versus challenger activity.

TALES, TRAPS AND TIPS
MICHAEL STEEN

Michael Steen has worked with Nike since 1995, and is a global leader at Nike Innovation. His job is to lead, manage and inspire the Global Apparel Innovation team, to enhance Nike's competitive edge.

ON EFFICIENCY IN GROWTH

An organisation shouldn't just become obsessed with innovation; it has to be obsessed with both efficiency and growth. When you scale, you need to understand how you unlock value from this. How do you reduce the costs of each unit?

The best organisations do this, as well as having the capability to think like scrappy entrepreneurs. The difficulty is flipping between the two; that's really hard. We have our boards, our governance, and our processes that are all set up in this way. I can apply the muscle of business as usual to maximise efficiency, but also have the capability to take risks on start-ups.

ON ACCOUNTING FOR INNOVATION

I'm a firm believer that the more that you embed P&L responsibilities into innovation, the more it brings the right level of accountability, responsibility and understanding.

ON FAILING

Failing is very much expected. It's embedded in everything we do, and it's needed to push those boundaries. You're designing, you're iterating. Absolutely critical to Nike is tinkering, engineering, playing around with stuff, mixing stuff. We have the funds and the capabilities, so we keep all this internal because anytime we unlock something, it's a competitive advantage to us.

ON PITCHING IDEAS

You can't bitch without a pitch.

THE PERILS OF GROWTH ADDICTION

YOU'VE ADOPTED THE SCALE-UP MINDSET, applied the ROCKET agenda to your growth board meetings, and overlaid just enough rigour on to the previously fluid start-up venture... but what if it still isn't working?

First, let's recognise the situation and how truly painful it is. Whether you're building this venture from scratch or have been handed the baton, it's still your 'baby', and any whiff of failure can come as an enormous personal blow. I refer you back to the unicorn myth and just how high the statistics are stacked against outright success.

But if you're not quite ready to throw in the towel, there are plenty of things to do to turn it around. Here are some tangible actions to get growth back on track:

TALK TO CUSTOMERS

➡ In conversations with customers, look for how they talk about their pain/problem, as well as how they talk about your idea or product. Explore the underlying intent behind their actions and claims.

➡ Aim for a broad mix: those who love your product and those who hate it, current buyers, those who never bought, and those no longer engaged in your business.

➡ Don't limit yourself to traditional research. There are huge untapped resources in customer services, on social media channels, or via retailers. Speaking to customers or even running a focus group isn't actually that hard and can be quite good fun.

ADJUST THE VALUE PROPOSITION

Redefine how customers gain value:

➡ Are they buying into you for the reasons you thought, or is it something else? Is there something else missing that would make your offer more compelling?

➡ Map the value proposition against the competition. How do you really stack up on points of difference or points of parity?

➡ Is the route to market right for your proposition and your audience? Are you reaching them where they're likely to purchase?

CHANGE THE TARGET AUDIENCE

Your product or service may already be a great solution to someone else's problem.

➡ Understand who your customers are. Talk to them. Are they who you were targeting or actually someone else? If they're slightly different, why is that? Might they be a better target than those who you initially designed your product for? What will you need to do differently?

➡ What tests can you run to see if your venture resonates more strongly with a different audience?

MIX UP THE COMMUNICATION

➡ Test changing the message hierarchy, wording, visuals or communication channels.

➡ Design a testing framework to understand the impact of each element in the communication.

➡ Map the purchase journey to see where the dropouts are occurring, and then focus tests on that.

Remember too, things fail. And often. Whether to hit stop or play is the point of difference between a failing business and a business that is failing to grow. Recognising innovation has potential, and maintaining the direction takes patience, determination and resilience. If the conditions allow, sticking with it is usually the best option.

STAYING NIMBLE BUT LEAPING HIGH

Growth is not just a continuation of Results. It is a period that demands a tangible shift in mindset. You need to lean into the future state and not just into innovation as an end in itself. It involves the application of rigour to bring order and build a business beyond innovation.

Whether the plan is to integrate the business into the mothership, spin it off or maintain the business as a unit, you must continue to innovate, and continue the cycle of FORGE. Your job isn't done; it's only really beginning. But next time, it may be easier. It certainly will be if you pick up the learnings from the next chapter.

Mechanisms such as 'growth boards' open you up to an outside world – to the value of looking beyond the venture itself. This is critical. After all, innovation and business live in the outside world. Customers don't buy exclusively into you or interact with your innovation in isolation; suppliers and talent don't work only with you; stakeholders such as investors or local government bodies work with multiple others. And, of course, in our digital world, every one of these is connected.

You and your innovation exist within a broad and dynamic Ecosystem. Your ability to navigate and benefit from the connections within an ecosystem will be a powerful driver of growth through scale-up and beyond. And it's to this Ecosystem we now turn our attention.

FORGE YOUR WAY

KEY TAKEAWAYS

➡ Scaling up requires a fundamental shift in mindset: what got us here, will not take us there.

➡ Every time the team grows by roughly 2.5× there is a noticeable shift in culture. Be ready for it.

➡ Growth boards can provide essential help along the scaling up journey. Ensure the conversation covers strategy, people, performance and projects by using ROCKET to frame your agenda.

➡ Embrace the good, the bad and the ugly in customer feedback. Make sure you hear it directly.

➡ Always make it better: keep testing, never stop iterating, and ensure every 'champion' campaign has a challenger-in-waiting.

QUESTIONS TO REFLECT ON

➡ What are your scale-up aims? Visualise what your business needs to look like at 2×, 5× and 10× revenue.

➡ How many of the senior team have talked directly with a customer in the last three months? And you?

➡ Are you maintaining your innovation ambidexterity? Can an innovation leader really break through process?

➡ Are all of your leading campaigns actively being challenged?

FREE RESOURCES

At www.entrepreneur-within.com/growth you'll find:

➡ Articles and videos dedicated to scaling a venture, with further innovation tales from those who have been there.

➡ A Growth Board toolkit with a ROCKET agenda template.

ECOSYSTEM

THE INNOVATION COMMUNITY

'If you want to go fast, go alone;
if you want to go far, go together.'
AFRICAN PROVERB

SO WE'VE REACHED THE FINAL element in our five-step FORGE methodology... but Ecosystem is not, I repeat, not the final step.

Unlike the previous elements, which are largely sequential (albeit with the opportunity for countless loop-backs), Ecosystem should be considered at all stages of the innovation journey. It wraps around everything we do.

Another key difference is our frame of reference. Focus, Originality, Results and Growth are designed to drive growth for a specific idea or innovation venture. Ecosystem is concerned with creating and sustaining the conditions for success. And not just for this venture but for all those that follow. Create the Ecosystem, and the rest will be much, much easier.

SO, WHAT'S AN 'ECOSYSTEM' ANYWAY?

It is a term imbued with a wide variety of meanings and ambiguity. British ecologist Arthur Tansley first coined it in 1935 to recognise the importance of transfers of materials between organisms and their environment. It was based on the fundamental belief that a community of organisms cannot be separated from their special environments.

Over the intervening years, businesses and government departments have appropriated it to apply to multiple disciplines and industries, yet each is rooted in the idea of interconnectivity. I find it helpful to think of an innovation ecosystem as an evolving network of companies, talent, and funding providers who collaborate intentionally to advance new business ventures.

In a hyperconnected world, this appears simply to represent common sense. The best innovations do not jump out of a vacuum, and if we return to our definition of innovation as 'forging previously unseen connections', then the greater exposure a business has to new connections, new stimulus and new resources, the greater the chances of success. Indeed, in an exact mirror of the natural world, survival would seem to depend on this very network.

Ecosystems are loosely defined networks. There is no top-down control, and no one person or organisation is responsible for every aspect of the ecosystem. This liberation from control is essential for the innovator to fully maximise the ecosystem's potential.

THE STORY OF
SILICON VALLEY

ONE OF THE GREAT BUSINESS ECOSYSTEMS in the world is Silicon Valley. Its magnetism is hard to resist for entrepreneurs wanting to establish a tech business.

Located in the southern part of the San Francisco Bay Area, Silicon Valley has a well-justified reputation for being the best place to start a new technology venture in the the world (it should be said that according to Startup Genome, London ties second place with New York City). This area is home to more than 2,000 tech companies, including Google, Meta, Apple, Netflix and PayPal.

There is an abundance of skilled workers wishing to get in early to the next unicorn. There is a well-established network of investors who are able to inject capital into all stages and who have experience investing in the tech sector. There is deep specialist knowledge from multiple nearby universities. There are strong entrepreneurial networks, including a wide range of resources for start-ups, incubators, accelerators and events for collaboration.

But why did Silicon Valley develop in the way it did? What can others learn from its development?

Up until the 1890s, the southern part of the Santa Clara Valley was best known for fruit trees and loads of them. And then, a railroad tycoon called Leland Stanford came along and founded Stanford University in 1885, welcoming its first student in 1891. This proved a pivotal point. The research coming out of the university was the most cutting-edge when it came to electronic products.

However, professors, including the dean of the school of engineering, Fredrick Terman, started to get frustrated because they noticed the good students were leaving the area. Terman decided to invest in businesses that committed to establishing themselves in the region and employing students from Stanford. The university leased land to technological firms. Two students in particular, Bill Hewlett and David Packard, under the fellowship of Terman, started the business in 1935 whose name you've already figured out. Other companies nurtured by Terman? Eastman Kodak, General Electric and Lockheed Corporation.

By the time of the Second World War, this area was known as a centre for electrical manufacturing. Ever forward-thinking, after the war, in 1951, the deans at Stanford University collaborated with the city of Palo Alto to create Stanford Industrial Park, 660 acres of research labs, manufacturing facilities and offices. It became all about the production of semiconductors. In particular, William Shockley believed that silicon was a better material for making transistors. He was right. Silicon Valley was born. And it grew up very quickly. The Space Race brought government funds to the area and venture capitalists and private equity quickly followed. It had the funding, the infrastructure, the legal firms, banks, and government support, and then, the personal computer hit. Microsoft, Apple, Oracle, Cisco, Adobe Systems.

The ecosystem is clear. However, it gets better. The people who founded these companies then invested in other ventures. Out of PayPal alone came: its founder Peter Thiel, the first outside investor in Facebook; Elon Musk, no need for an explanation here, and others who founded YouTube, Yammer, Yelp, Kiva, LinkedIn, to name a few.

And it just keeps growing and growing. It all comes together to develop a flywheel, whereby if you develop a venture in Silicon Valley, you've got so many more advantages than if you develop it elsewhere. But it doesn't have to be about location.

BEYOND GEOGRAPHY

There are many examples of business ecosystems being defined by places, but ecosystems do not need to be geographical. Physical proximity has obvious advantages, but so do product-led ecosystems whereby companies come together to solve a problem. Ecosystems could be centred around a platform, too: a shopping centre, Amazon, Vimeo.

What better example than the ground-breaking pace of Covid-19 vaccine development, which crossed global boundaries, leveraged investment from multiple governments and organisations, and connected thinking from academics and front-line medics? Yes, it was developed around a very specific solution at a very specific time, but it has paved the way for a new approach to vaccine development and virus reactivity. It's a great example of a product-based ecosystem.

Informal or formal, business and innovation ecosystems tend to generate from an anchor point. That could be an established company starting to reach out, a university, an investment fund or even local government. These 'anchors' are typically well known, committed to the cause, and financially stable enough to support complementary efforts. Alongside the geographic ecosystem, you'll find them centred around a product or a platform. Let's delve into how different ecosystems function around a common 'why', a unifying purpose.

PRODUCT-BASED ECOSYSTEM

A product-based ecosystem revolves around a core product that acts as the primary anchor. The focus is on the product itself, its features, and potential accessories.

An ecosystem based around a single product often involves a network of companies that are all trying to enhance the usability, performance or customer experience of the core product and to make money for their troubles.

Think about the Apple iPhone. As a core product by itself, the iPhone is certainly a wonderful specimen of engineering and design excellence. But without the many apps, accessories and services, the value proposition would not be anywhere near as compelling as it is with them.

Product-based ecosystems can evolve wherever the core 'product' is the primary focus but where other products, services or experiences can add significant value. Think of the ecosystem that would develop around a large-scale infrastructure project – such as a new high-speed railway line. Imagine all the services and products that need to be involved to ensure the ultimate passenger experience.

PLATFORM-BASED ECOSYSTEM

A platform-based ecosystem isn't a new idea. It's a network that sprouts from a central platform. It's a place where interactions happen, where transactions take place, and where more products and services can be sold. The platform acts as the foundation to enable other players in the ecosystem to create value. The more players and interactions, the more valuable the ecosystem is for everyone.

A great example is Amazon Web Services (AWS), which is a cloud computing platform at its core. It provides computing power, storage facilities, apps and machine learning tools, among other things. Yet the value is magnified by enabling third-party software and consulting partners to add to the overall value proposition. The more services, software and partnerships there are, the more value there is for everyone involved.

A shopping centre would be an example of a 'real-world' platform-based ecosystem. The shopping centre provides the physical space and infrastructure for various retail stores, entertainment venues, restaurants and other services to operate. The more footfall to the shopping centre, the more value can be created for everyone.

In short, you can buy a product from a product-based ecosystem (an iPhone, garden furniture, a can of beer), but you can't buy a platform such as a shopping centre or a web service. Either way, the benefits of being an integral part of an ecosystem are clear.

WHY YOU NEED TO BE PART OF AN ECOSYSTEM

Being part of an ecosystem enables the survival not just of one species but of the entire collection of diverse species; it's exactly what nature intended. It helps to reduce the risk associated with doing new things while at the same time increasing the likelihood of success. Look beyond the immediate goals and lean into an ecosystem.

ACCESS TO RESOURCES

An ecosystem enables access to the broadest possible range of resources and inputs required for success. We'll discuss the components below, but this includes talent, knowledge, funding and networks.

Without the right resources, growth is hard. Tapping into an ecosystem that already exists is a massive risk reducer because the conditions are already in place to give your venture an immediate leg up. As the business develops, acting within the ecosystem is also the surest way to create the conditions for ongoing growth. It's not just your current product or service; future innovations will also benefit.

EXTERNAL VALIDATION

An ecosystem brings critical fresh thinking from beyond the organisation, which can help shape the innovation via real-world inputs. It also avoids the fatal echo chamber effect, where an idea is reinforced as a good idea without any more analytical thought.

There's no better way to clarify what your innovation is about than having to explain it to others, especially when you need to engage their support. The value-add of operating in an ecosystem with multiple – sometimes competing – viewpoints hones a proposition far better than any development in-house is ever likely to achieve. The stimulus of different ideas and perspectives can shine a completely new light on the problem to drive sharper ways of thinking about the solutions.

COLLABORATION AND COMPETITION

All the companies mentioned in our Silicon Valley story were neighbours. Competition is a motor for innovation. And when it's on your doorstep, you up your game and that of the ecosystem. But the right collaboration can prove very beneficial. It's actually essential for most businesses. Within an ecosystem, you'll find like-minded and complementary businesses, all working towards the same purpose. Whether it's component parts, legal expertise, funding or marketing, chances are you'll find exactly what you need within a mature ecosystem. This might even offer new partnership opportunities.

SHARED LEARNINGS AND INSPIRATION

The ecosystem will be a source of inspiration. It's like a continuous conference, and the more you put in, the more you'll get out of it. It should be a network that shares learnings, experience and advice. It should be a place of inspiration where ideas can bounce around, kept afloat by enthusiastic members.

TALES, TRAPS AND TIPS
EVE ROODHOUSE

*Eve Roodhouse has worked at
NHS Digital leading change, and as
the Chief Officer of Leeds City Council.
She is now leading on Public Sector Reform
at the Local Government Association.*

ON ANCHOR NETWORKS

We established the initial anchors network for Leeds, which is
focused on the large institutions in the city that are not going to
leave. That includes the council, the NHS, the universities and the
Further Education sector. Working together they can really move
the dial on delivering inclusive economic growth.

ON THE IMPORTANCE OF INNOVATION NETWORKS

Innovation is really important for places and for the public sector,
because collectively we face massive challenges that we must
resolve. You're not going to tackle health inequalities, low pay or
the climate emergency without working with others to innovate,
with the private sector, universities, with risk capital, and other
partners all at the table together.

ON INNOVATING FOR THE GREATER GOOD

We need to create an innovation ecosystem focused on supporting
people who want to solve these big societal challenges. By
embedding the innovation vision within the inclusive growth
strategy in Leeds we created an intentional link signalling to
everybody what the city stands for and what we want to achieve for
our people working with our partners.

ON INNOVATION IN UNIVERSITIES

We had universities involved at the start. Students work alongside
people in law and tech. Interaction happens between people that
otherwise wouldn't meet.

NAVIGATING ECOSYSTEMS WITHIN LARGE CORPORATIONS

IT'S NOT ALL ON THE OUTSIDE

Ecosystems aren't restricted to external systems with connections, knowledge and resource flows. For large organisations, an internal ecosystem itself is a powerful starting point to be tapped into and fostered.

Large corporations do initiate innovation hubs, teams and projects, and empower plenty of individuals. The problem is that successfully navigating them from one corner of the organisation is almost impossible. Amazon employs 1.5 million people. Finding the right person or team in an organisation that employs more people than the population of Estonia isn't always straightforward. And how often do those hubs, teams, projects and individuals fully reach out beyond their immediate objectives and business unit to other parts of the business doing the same? Typically and regretfully, the answer is almost never. And yet, within a single organisation, a little digging unearths pockets of innovation dotted everywhere.

IT'S NOT ALL ON THE INSIDE

The danger in the point above is that, for those working in a large organisation, it's easy to think there is less need to participate actively in an external ecosystem.

Large companies have so many more resources than start-ups, and it's easy to fall prey to the belief that you're leveraging external thinking just by reaching out to colleagues in a different function.

Working and collaborating externally is notoriously difficult for large organisations (if in doubt, just try purchasing something from a start-up and watch how the well-intentioned procurement processes close it down). Thankfully, there are signs of change and evidence that the insular mindset is shifting, largely thanks to the open innovation movement.

In fact, according to the Sopra Steria Open Innovation Report from 2023, 72 per cent of European companies now claim to be running collaboration projects with start-ups, and 67 per cent claim that collaboration with start-ups is either important or mission-critical to their strategy.

Despite all that, it remains unclear exactly what proportion of innovation projects within corporations actually connect with the outside world. Interviews with internal innovators are still too frequently full of tales of navigating internal bureaucracy, and in my experience, many privately admit to not knowing where to start when it comes to reaching out into the unknown.

This matters. The risk of groupthink within a large organisation is all too real; nobody gets fired for repeating what the CEO said, and yet the potential for thinking within a vacuum – thereby stifling the real potential of innovation – is immense. But what if there was a way of making innovation efforts visible and connectable across the organisation? Could tech be leveraged to make connections seamless and in real-time?

Also, ask how your organisation would overcome its squeamishness regarding the sharing of knowledge or put in place the right guardrails to allow knowledge flow. Assessing what is genuine commercially sensitive IP versus imagined is key. Think about NDAs and contractual obligations as external organisations would do.

Below, we'll examine how to unlock ecosystems, but let's first look at the composite parts of an innovation ecosystem.

THE COMPONENTS OF AN INNOVATION ECOSYSTEM

AN ECOSYSTEM, BY ITS NATURE, is an amorphous mass, a collection of wildly diverse elements that create the conditions for success across the entire environment. That said, we can discern the essential components of an innovation ecosystem in a way that, practically, you can see your strengths as well as the gaps you need to fill. Let's reiterate again that the ecosystem should be thought about from the very beginning of any new venture. I find it helpful to break down the components of an ecosystem into four key areas: Knowledge, Funding, Networks and Talent. There are nuances, of course, but tapping into those fundamental sections will make life much easier.

THE CENTRE OF THE ECOSYSTEM

At the heart of every ecosystem are the innovators, the ones who make things happen. These are intrapreneurs. In Silicon Valley, it would be the superstars Peter Thiel, Elon Musk and Bill Gates. Through their curiosity, vision and drive for change, they can act as a magnetic force that helps to hold the ecosystem in place around the problem. The benefits of being at the centre of an ecosystem are clear.

This idea is neatly wrapped up in a model known as an 'entrepreneurship acceleration cycle'. A clumsy title, but the concept is simple. As the entrepreneur or intrapreneur, you have the ambition (and key here is the word 'ambition') to build a scalable venture, one that innovates and thrives, one

that has long-term sustainable growth as a goal. Go big.

Because you are part of an ecosystem, the components of which we'll examine below, you have access to talent, knowledge, finance and networks. This compounding effect enables growth and tips the odds of becoming successful in your favour.

For those who are successful, there is the opportunity to pay back. This ecosystem that helped nurture you, is now looking to you for help. New companies are starting around you, new suppliers are getting involved. If you've succeeded, it's rewarding to commit to help others, and not retire to a tax haven with a nice beach but little else happening. You stay in the area; you support new companies, and you nurture new talent. You become the mentor; you start a new business. Your first eight employees, after all, have started their own and to great success. It works for you and everyone else involved. And it requires giving back.

ECOSYSTEM MATURITY MATRIX

FOR THOSE INTERESTED in helping to curate an ecosystem, understanding how mature the key components are is incredibly helpful when determining where to connect or what additional resources might need to be invited in.

I've found it helpful to visualise the development of an ecosystem using the maturity matrix. The table below explains more, but in brief, the five levels of ecosystem maturity are as follows.

➡ **Emerging.** A convergence around a problem or opportunity area is developing, and the players are keen to understand how they might start to collaborate.

➡ **Aspiring.** There are some important foundations in place, alongside an ambition to develop wider partnerships.

➡ **Progressive.** A well-defined ecosystem is in place, and participants are starting to feel the benefits as the ecosystem begins to take on a life of its own.

➡ **Strategic.** There is a recognised cluster in place with clear links to broader economic priorities, and well-defined success stories have emerged.

➡ **Transformative.** These ecosystems are part of the global elite, which attracts global talent, investment and high profile entrepreneurs.

	EMERGING	ASPIRING	PROGRESSIVE	STRATEGIC	TRANSFORMATIVE
INNOVATORS	Solo founders often isolated and unstructured, with limited collaboration.	Multiple small teams, with occasional collaborative projects.	Diverse and maturing innovative ventures, with a collaborative programme taking shape (e.g. innovation labs).	Cross-sector collaborations, with established networks between corporates and start-ups (with successful outcomes).	Global thought leaders, pioneering market transformations and industry-leading innovations.
CAPITAL PROVIDERS	Sporadic access to capital from individual investors, often with limited funding; minimal business loan availability.	Growing interest and activity from local investors, some angel networks and debt funding options.	Diverse sector base, with active angel investor groups and private equity, local government support and structured credit facilities.	Strong multi-faceted investment sources; international investors and access to venture capitals and numerous structured finance options.	Comprehensive and competitive funding ecosystem with globally connected investment networks and sophisticated banking services.
EXPERTISE PROVIDERS	Limited local expertise, sporadic and informal knowledge sharing.	Growing pool of regional experts, increasing academic-industry partnerships and emerging mentor processes.	Strong regional expertise, established academic-industry collaborations, well-equipped facilities for R7D and infrastructure for knowledge sharing.	Nationally recognised experts, extensive collaborations between academia and industry leading to investible propositions.	Global hub of expertise, with state-of-the-art facilities for innovation. Leading international research collaborations.
TALENT PROVIDERS	Basic education facilities, limited industry-specific talent pipeline; support functions under-developed.	Developing education infrastructure, growing talent pool; support for entrepreneurs and high growth business scaling.	Established education systems with speciality tracks, strong local talent in key industries; growing support ecosystem for high-growth businesses.	Internationally recognised training programmes, deep and diverse pool of specialised talent; robust mentoring enabling serial entrepreneurs and rapid business scaling.	Global talent magnet, renowned for top-tier educational and training institutions; world-class support services for entrepreneurs and high-growth enterprises.
NETWORK PROVIDERS	Few networking events, limited community engagement with nascent and informal networks.	Growing number of regional networking events, emerging incubators and accelerators enabling collaboration.	Regular, diverse networking events and community initiatives across all stakeholder groups with public sector support.	Frequent high-profile events attracting national attention. Strong active networking communities with governmant support and corporate participation.	Globally recognised events drawing international participation and shaping government policy. Dynamic networks fostering global networks to define industry standards.

TALENT

Access to talent is often cited as one of the largest barriers to business growth. However, as ecosystems develop around a particular sector or specialism, they become a hub for related businesses and naturally attract a larger pool of skilled professionals looking for opportunities in this field. This critical mass of skills and expertise propels high-growth ventures. Talent falls into two camps: Foundational and Specialist.

Foundational talent includes the founders and the early team who deliver the operations and build a company culture. These are the ones who are full-time on the project, who have the best interests of the innovation at heart, and who will be laser-guided in making it succeed. The foundational team become generalists with a unique insight into all the facets of the business; they can turn their hand to most things.

There's also the need for specialist talent and expert contributors who can offer high impact. Ecosystems often forge strong links with further and higher education establishments as well as other training providers, which can offer a concentration of specialist knowledge and skills. Think fractional CFOs, CTOs or CROs, or any other confusing acronym with 'chief' at the beginning. This, in turn, helps accelerate new product development and deepen knowledge and expertise in the field.

KNOWLEDGE

Information and insights help underpin all innovation. The wider you look, the more voices you hear, and the more chances of success you'll have. There are two types of knowledge to look at here: Technical knowledge and growth knowledge.

Technical knowledge is the specific expertise that powers product development and R&D for ventures operating in a technical or knowledge-intensive space. This group could include university researchers as well as seasoned professionals who have worked in expert disciplines with similar businesses. They can provide deep insights, access to technical research and offer specialised skills to help overcome challenges.

Having trusted people around you who have done it before is priceless. This is what I call 'growth knowledge'. That acquired wisdom, through start-up and scale-up phases, is hard-earned and endlessly valuable. It also brings credible validation to your venture outside of the echo chamber and it is earned with genuine knowledge.

FUNDING

Thriving ecosystems attract a wider variety of funding sources, including angel investors, venture capital, banks and government grants tailored to support emerging technologies. This will range from those offering seed funding to help get a new business off the ground to those capable of writing larger cheques to help scale growth. Within a large business, you'll likely find corporate venture capital available to units within and outside businesses.

What you are ideally looking for are people and organisations to offer more than simply monetary support. Strategic guidance and, most importantly, access to valuable networks. And while this group may not be there from the very start, you'll need to build an ecosystem of these sources if the ventures are to take off.

For corporate ventures, the capital providers will typically be an internal budget holder allocated to an innovation project, often with strategic clout at the board level. But to be clear, this doesn't mean that venture products and services in corporations shouldn't look for external funding. VCs and angel investors might be just as interested in these kinds of ventures if they are deemed too risky for the larger business.

You'll need to balance growth capital with working capital to fuel rapid expansion. This funding can open doors for more ambitious projects. There's also a requirement for operational funding, the working capital to support day-to-day business, and to enable cash flow commitments to be met.

NETWORKS

An ecosystem needs connectors and people to bring everything together. The connectors that bring the ecosystem together are hard to define, but they are the very foundation of an ecosystem. They are the bees that pollinate the garden. It could take the form of business incubators and accelerators or perhaps individuals who can connect you to talent, funding, regulation and developers. Or perhaps sector-specific media and support organisations can help businesses stay up-to-date with emerging trends and technologies. These systems help facilitate knowledge-sharing and provide vital introductions to new and existing members. They provide platforms for networking, mentorship and exposure, helping to engineer an environment that links all players in the ecosystem. How these players show up and interact is entirely fluid and varies from one ecosystem to another. This tight web of relationships is hard to untangle and understand thoroughly. Pollination is directly related to the effort that is put in. The connectors within an ecosystem help build a community focused on solving a problem. Consider too the conditions to facilitate networks, the physical locations, the events, the forums. Is it a coffee shop, an innovation lab, a networking event, something virtual?

Think too of a community of passionate consumers, those who clearly believe in the mission. They are invaluable and will go a long way to make the venture a success. If you have a tribe of consumers who love and follow everything you do, they provide an extraordinary resource within your ecosystem. You can build things with them and use their expertise for testing. They'll tell you how to improve the product or service. They are your most valuable advocates and learning resource. They also help you access new markets and introduce you to adjacent businesses. They have their ear on the ground. Bring them in.

It's probably pretty clear – given the amorphous and dynamic nature of ecosystems – that there are no hard and fast rules for how to get involved. If you're new to innovation, the whole idea is probably somewhat daunting. And if you're running fast to nurture a shining new idea, then frankly, when do you have the time or headspace to even think about it?

When we set out on our Beer Hawk journey we certainly hadn't thought about any of this. We were almost 100 per cent focused on making the idea work and getting actual beer into actual customers' hands. And yet, over time (and in particular, once we came up for air after our first Christmas rush), we found ourselves participating in a number of networks that helped us drive the business to the scale it eventually achieved. There was undoubtedly some level of accident and luck along the way, but also, when I look back, some definite behaviours and approaches that made this happen.

The vast majority of us do not reside in or anywhere near Silicon Valley or one of its global equivalents. So, chances are that the existing ecosystems will be significantly less obvious and, therefore, potentially more difficult to penetrate. But there are some practical steps we can deploy to get going and apply ecosystem theory to our innovation ventures inside and outside a big corporation.

COMMIT TO COLLABORATE

You'll never get started if you don't buy into the value of being part of an ecosystem. You have to have the curiosity, develop the confidence to go looking, and be generous to give more than you take. Once you embrace the mindset that growth will come from being part of something bigger than yourself, then you're setting the wheels in motion.

TALES, TRAPS AND TIPS
MARTIN STOW

Dr Martin Stow is the Pro-Vice Chancellor for Business Engagement and Enterprise at the University of Leeds, with significant business leadership experience across the medical device and diagnostics industry. He has led R&D within multinational healthcare companies such as Johnson & Johnson, as well as leading start-up organisations.

ON THE SCALING MINDSET

Many companies reach a significant size but struggle to get beyond that. They plateau because growing further often requires a total mindset shift. Often, it will be entrepreneurs who are very good at the early stage – concept testing, establishing a marketplace or a presence – but scaling requires a different mindset and skillset. Unfortunately, these scale-ups don't often get the right level of support and help, which is a real shame as this is often the point where you can really make an impact relatively quickly.

ON CREATING TIME FOR INNOVATION

At Johnson & Johnson, we tried to enable 20 per cent of a researcher's time to be spent on innovation. They can decide the area to spend this time on, but there's a framework to work within. We cut out all of the approval processes and bureaucracy and enabled the team to decide what to do. We tried to create space, to empower people to go out into the real world, to understand real challenges for healthcare professionals and patients, and to start thinking about innovating around that.

ON CREATING SPACE FOR INNOVATION

My tip would be around how organisations can create space for people to innovate. Time needs to be spent on understanding customer needs. Create space and give scientists and engineers an opportunity to connect to the end user in a different way.

ON THE POWER OF ECOSYSTEMS

A university is uniquely positioned to bring together the right stakeholders to spur on innovation and to start thinking differently. There is a leadership and convening role which is really powerful for driving both economic and societal change in the city and region.

ON REINVESTING BACK INTO THE ECOSYSTEM

When companies have scaled, the initial founders and early investors can often realise some of that capital and reinvest it into new companies within the region. The knowledge and expertise that they bring can often be as valuable as the money. This cycle helps to create a sustainable, self-fulfilling system, which happens in the best innovation ecosystems.

ON OPENING UP THE CORPORATION

Corporations can often be too closed and risk averse. They can get hung up over intellectual property and confidentiality, and they can quickly come up with 1,000 reasons why they can't do something, as opposed to saying, 'Well, let's just go for it.' If there's an ecosystem that the corporation trusts and gets to know players within that – academics, entrepreneurs – then it's much easier to say, 'Let's just do this.' Everybody's going to benefit.

ON MANAGING EXPECTATIONS OF LEADERSHIP

One of the biggest traps in a corporation is not managing the expectations of senior leadership, particularly around the time it takes to research and develop a new product. This requires commitment and foresight in the long term. Without this understanding and trust on the part of the leadership team then decisions can be made in the short term which are detrimental to the longer term goal and in reality inhibit innovation.

MAKE TIME

Finding time to participate in networks is so difficult to achieve. The time away from the 'day job' has an immediate impact, while the positive return on this time can feel pretty far-off and vague. But it's the same principle as any to-do list; you need to find the balance, the 'urgent' and the 'important'. If not, you'll only ever do what's urgent and not what's important.

Make time to build connections, attend events, visit organisations, join groups, explore and be prepared to do the same in return because only then will you start to make real connections in the ecosystems around you.

MAP IT OUT

Drawing out a map of an entire ecosystem can feel an impossible ask when you're new to all this. How do I know who to connect with? Where should I go? Start with a list of the key players and ask them to add to the list. Identify the kinds of connections and partners that you might need. At this point, looking back at the ecosystem elements illustration can help. It can help you map out whom you have access to and, crucially, where the gaps are.

Make sure you include internal and external connections in your ecosystem map. See where the current level of maturity sits and what gaps stand out. Then, it's time to start spinning the wheel, make an action plan and start talking to people. It doesn't take long for a few tentative connections to become a network.

Within a large organisation, you'll often find innovation happening in many places. The problem is that it's utterly disconnected. Connecting the innovation dots is up to you. Plant a huge flag in the ground, wave it cheerfully, and make it easy for other people to find you. Most teams are working within their own virtual worlds with little to no visibility of what's going on beyond. But what if there are ways of making innovation efforts visible across the organisation? Make it easy for others to engage in the ecosystem.

LEARN FROM OTHERS

It's easy to forget that you're unlikely to be the first one round this block. You might be new to your particular problem–solution, but there will be plenty of others who are not. Seek out those who have experience – in your field or adjacent – and use them to guide you and introduce you to the wider world.

You'll be amazed how generous people are with their time in the world of entrepreneurship. This is not simply a philanthropic gesture; in the true spirit of ecosystems, you never quite know how paying it forward might play out and whether the support might well pay back indirectly over time.

Within a large organisation, mentorship could take the form of people who have done it before. However, the reality for many large organisations is that they do leverage external expertise and perspectives – just look at the board and the shareholders – but they often exist at a very senior level, and are inaccessible to many of those actually doing the work.

SPIN THE WHEEL

Helping to develop a comprehensive ecosystem and being aware of the advantages and gaps within it, can become your most important tool. An established ecosystem will give the toolkits of Focus, Originality, Results and Growth significantly more chance for success. Keep the ecosystem spinning, keep the members engaged, keep being generous yourself, and the ecosystem for innovation will continuously develop, mature and grow. Now, look back to the previous chapters and apply the benefits of Ecosystem to each.

Focus: Are there mentors who can help guide you towards the right problem? Are there people who will help hone your vision? Can you learn from similar businesses to understand the potential market? Has a university or government organisation done the homework for you? Are industry papers available to help understand the value chain?

Originality: What compatible offerings are within your ecosystem? Can you collaborate with external organisations to improve your supply chain, service or product? Is there a university working on solving a similar problem? Is there a branding agency particularly adept at telling similar stories?

Results: Is there a group you can tap into for quick feedback on prototypes? Are there existing organisations out there? Is there a friendly company that has done some of the learning for you? Has an organisation already assessed the market and gathered intelligence?

Growth: Has anyone gone through this stage before? Is there talent with growth experience who you can learn from? Who would bring expertise to your growth board? Are there systems that other companies use to great effect?

FORGE YOUR WAY

KEY TAKEAWAYS

➡ Ecosystems can be the multiplier that increase
the likelihood of innovation success.

➡ An innovation ecosystem is an evolving network of
companies, talent and funding providers who collaborate
intentionally to advance new business ventures.

➡ These ecosystems can be geographically-focused,
product-based or platform-based; but ecosystems
will be at varying levels of maturity.

➡ Large corporations have incredible resources,
but the danger with having so much on the inside
is not participating in what's available on the outside.

QUESTIONS TO REFLECT ON

➡ What ecosystems are you part of, internally or externally?
How mature are they?

➡ Have you mapped out your own innovation ecosystem?

➡ What do you currently bring to the ecosystems
you're part of? What do you want to get out of them?

➡ Go back through all your notes on Focus, Originality, Results
and Growth and look at them through the prism of your
ecosystem. How can the ecosystem help with every area?

FREE RESOURCES

At www.entrepreneur-within.com/ecosystem you'll find:

➡ Guides explaining how to develop an ecosystem along
the maturity matrix, with real-world examples.

➡ A free and downloadable infographic on ecosystem
components.

FORGE YOUR OWN PATH

FORGE YOUR OWN PATH

NOW IT'S OVER TO YOU. It's your turn to forge your own
path. To embark on your own quest. Great, great things
can come from innovation, and the more you exercise
that innovation muscle, the more you embed it in your
organisation. Rarely in the field of human innovation has
the protagonist acted alone. We know the names of the
people who invented the steam engine and the car, the
incandescent light bulb and the aeroplane. We know the
names behind the personal computer and the smartphone,
the World Wide Web, space travel and the printing press.
None acted alone. None of these ideas fell out of the sky.

Look also, at the great companies of the twenty-first
century. Those who are changing our lives for the better.
OpenAI, Amazon, Apple, Pfizer, Maersk, Walmart, Airbnb,
Sony, Nike, Patagonia, Revolut... No one acted alone to
build these companies, no matter the pedestal we put some
founders on. They continued to innovate. Again and again.

These companies, and thousands more you could add
to this list, did not find the magic bullet and hit success on
day one. Not one. What they did have – and this is the tenet
of this book – is the combination of the entrepreneurial
mindset AND the efficient processes of big business.
Creativity abounded among the machinery of big business.

The entrepreneurial mindset: focus, originality, effective
re-evaluation. The business mindset: efficiency, process,
funding, profit. Companies must bring these aspects
together to thrive. Those that don't will disappear.

The FORGE methodology is designed to help bring these opposing forces together. Every company is different, every product different, and every innovator-in-chief is different, but the FORGE methodology pulls together the common threads to achieve sustainable, innovation-led growth within an organisation.

You, our intrapreneur, have a great advantage. You have access to funding, to expertise, to knowledge, to markets, to science, which a start-up entrepreneur could only dream of.

Your job, your single job, is to realise that. To ensure this unfair advantage does not turn into complacency, or get strangled by red tape. To harness the great benefits of organisations – no matter the size – and embed the entrepreneurial mindset. Give yourself permission to dream, give your team and your bosses permission to dream, and dream big.

Combining true innovation with the power of business is the most powerful force on earth. There are a handful of companies who achieve this. Now imagine if every company, from Abuja to Tehran, New York to London, Leeds to Buenos Aires, Kuala Lumpur to Canberra, could harness this power.

Right now, there are ideas about to emerge that are going to change the world. There are innovations that will alter the way we think, as the smartphone did. There are innovations that will change the way we shop, that will improve lifespans, that will bring clean water to billions, and that will address the great problem of our day: climate change. There are innovations in development right now that will lead us into periods of great uncertainty and change. AI is already doing it. We know it will force us to ask questions because there has always been something. The printing press,

the spinning jenny, the compass, birth control, nuclear power, batteries, pasteurisation and vaccines. Again, none of these innovations came from nowhere. Decades of work, decades of minor breakthroughs, of single-minded focus. Decades of allowing the space for creativity, decades of continuous testing, decades of building the foundations, decades of developing the network of knowledge, power, finance and audiences.

I've offered you the toolkit. *The Entrepreneur Within* is a reference book, one designed to be scribbled in, one designed to be well thumbed. I want to see it with coffee stains and ideas jotted down in the margins. In it, I've combined my personal learnings with those from the people who have inspired me. I hope it will save you years of learning.

As I said in the introduction, there's never been a better time to innovate. Ever.

Now it's over to you.

What are you going to do today?

FURTHER RESOURCES

MAKE THE FORGE FRAMEWORK WORK FOR YOU
Throughout this book, we've pointed you in the direction
of free resources, templates and inspiration that can be
found at www.entrepreneur-within.com. To access exclusive
content for readers of this book, snap the QR code below.
In addition to these resources, you'll find our podcast,
articles that inspire and give real-life advice, plus interviews
with some of the world's most innovative business people.

TAKE THE FORGE DIAGNOSTIC
At www.entrepreneur-within.com you can also take our
FORGE Diagnostic to discover your hidden strengths
and help identify areas of FORGE – Focus, Originality,
Results, Growth, Ecosystem – we can help you improve to
accelerate your innovation-led growth. It just takes a few
minutes, but you'll save invaluable time and energy.

Use this QR code to find exclusive content.

ENDNOTES

THROUGHOUT THIS BOOK, I've tried to reference as many sources as possible within the text itself. There are some concepts, though, that warrant further explanation, comment or pointing to additional resources and these are referenced here:

1. THE BUSINESS LIFE CYCLE – PAGES 24–25
There have been many expressions of a five-stage business life cycle, but I took my initial inspiration from the *Harvard Business Review* (May 1983) and added my own fire-related descriptors. The average company age of 8.6 years is based on UK Companies House data. The 'S-Curve' referenced on these pages is also not a new concept, but first applied by Charles Handy in his excellent book *The Empty Raincoat: Making Sense of the Future*, first edition, New York City, NY: Random House, 1995.

2. INNOVATION FRONTIERS – PAGE 30
I developed my thinking based on *The Innovation Ambition Matrix*, Nagji, B., & Tuff, G. (2012), *Harvard Business Review*. I also referred to McKinsey's Three Horizons of Innovation, initially published in December 2009. I find these two very helpful in separating the differences in ambition and determining where ownership for new innovation should sit within an organisation.

3. IMPORTANCE OF INNOVATION – PAGE 32
McKinsey provides some excellent insight and analysis on innovation. This particular statistic was taken from a McKinsey Global Survey back in 2010, and can be found in the article 'Innovation and commercialization, 2010: McKinsey Global Survey results.'

4. THE INNOVATOR'S DILEMMA – PAGE 42
Clayton Christensen (1952–2020) was an American academic and consultant. He wrote *The Innovator's Dilemma: When New Technologies Cause Great Firms to Fail* back in 1997, which developed his theory on disruptive innovation. It's well worth a read, especially for those in a large incumbent company.

5. PRODUCT-MARKET FIT – PAGE 67

Andy Rachleff, the co-founder of Benchmark Capital, is credited with originally coining the term 'product-market fit' (PMF), who defined it as 'a unique product offering that people desperately want'. Rachleff in turn gives a lot of credit for the initial thinking to Don Valentine, the Founder of Sequoia Capital. When setting out on a new innovation venture, arguably, finding PMF is the single most important thing. I like to use the Sean Ellis score, which asks, 'How would you feel if you could no longer use [product]?' If at least 40 per cent of your users would answer 'Very disappointed' it's a strong indication that you have achieved PMF.

6. IKIGAI – PAGE 88

I have found the concept of *Ikigai* extremely useful both in my own businesses and in coaching entrepreneurs and CEOs. The book *Ikigai: The Japanese secret to a long and happy life* has been very helpful in exploring this concept further, and I would recommend adding it to your reading list.

7. EDWARD DE BONO – PAGE 107

I had the pleasure of sitting next to Edward De Bono for a long dinner back in 2005. By then, I was already working with his techniques to inspire innovation at P&G, and we had the chance to discuss his theories and models at length. I found his 'Rivers of Thinking' theory about the workings of the brain very powerful.

8. POWER LAW – PAGE 131

In statistics, a power law is a functional relationship between two quantities. I'm specifically referring to my understanding of an investing power law, which I've seen at play in venture capital. Here, one single investment can yield returns greater than all other investments combined, often by orders of magnitude. Returns are not evenly distributed.

9. BOYD'S LAW OF ITERATION – PAGE 139

John Boyd, a military strategist and pilot, developed this theory about iterative cycles of decision-making and action. It can often be summarised as 'speed of iteration beats the quality of iteration'. I've seen this hold true time and time again.

10. DVF – PAGE 142

IDEO, a global design company, conceptualised the design thinking methodology, which included using desirability, viability, and feasibility as a framework to test ideas. Excellent resources can be found at https://designthinking.ideo.com

ACKNOWLEDGEMENTS

I NEVER INTENDED TO WRITE A BOOK. Had I known how time-consuming and difficult it was, I doubt I'd have ever started. I would say the same about my business. It wasn't simply naive optimism that got me through, but the help and support from so many people. And coffee. Lots of coffee.

Let me start my thanks at home. This book wouldn't exist without the endless patience and love I've received from my wife Michelle and my three wonderful children, Sam, Philippa and Catherine. Thanks for keeping the faith (and also for reminding me when I drone on too much about it!).

Special mentions must go to my good friends who collaborated with me on this project. To Richard Pascoe, my invaluable companion, as we ventured on our first-time author journey together. To Daniel Neilson, my amazing editor who has the most helpful knack of cutting me off just at the right time. To Chris Day, my illustrator-in-chief, whose expressive graphics bring the words to life.

Thank you to the team at Unicorn Publishing, who believed in the initial vision for this book and delivered the book that's in our hands today. And a warm-hearted thank you to everyone who provided their innovation tale for this book – whether included in this final version or not, it's helped shape my thinking about how innovation happens in the real world. I'll always be grateful to the beta readers who took such time and care to review my early drafts and just made them so much better. Especially to Meldrum, Steve, Richard, Rob and Saul, who phrased their feedback in ways that forced me to think differently.

Innovation is a team game. Thanks to everyone who has been part of the journey with me. I can't wait to see where we go next...

INDEX

Published in 2025 by Unicorn,
an imprint of Unicorn Publishing Group
Charleston Studio
Meadow Business Centre
Lewes BN8 5RW
www.unicornpublishing.org

Every effort has been made to trace copyright holders and to obtain
their permission for the use of copyright material. The publisher
apologises for any errors or omissions and would be grateful if notified
of any corrections that should be incorporated in future reprints or
editions of this book.

ISBN 978-1-917458-09-2

10 9 8 7 6 5 4 3 2 1

Illustrations by Chris Day, Little Creature Ltd
Design by Felicity Price-Smith
Edited by Daniel Neilson
Printed in Scotland by Bell & Bain Ltd